JOURNAL FOR THE STUDY OF THE OLD TESTAMENT
SUPPLEMENT SERIES
# 78

*Editors*
David J A Clines
Philip R Davies

BIBLE AND LITERATURE SERIES
# 21

*General Editor*
David M. Gunn

*Assistant General Editor*
Danna Nolan Fewell

*Consultant Editors*
Elizabeth Struthers Malbon
James G. Williams

Almond Press
Sheffield

# Swallowing the Scroll

### Textuality and the Dynamics
### of Discourse in Ezekiel's Prophecy

Ellen F. Davis

The Almond Press · 1989

Bible and Literature Series, 21

*General Editor*: David M. Gunn
(Columbia Theological Seminary, Decatur, Georgia)
*Assistant General Editor*: Danna Nolan Fewell
(Perkins School of Theology, Dallas, Texas)
*Consultant Editors*: Elizabeth Struthers Malbon
(Virginia Polytechnic Institute & State University, Blacksburg, Virginia)
James G. Williams
(Syracuse University, Syracuse, New York)

Published by Almond Press
Editorial direction: David M. Gunn
Columbia Theological Seminary
P.O. Box 520, Decatur
GA 30031, U.S.A.
Almond Press is an imprint of
Sheffield Academic Press Ltd
The University of Sheffield
343 Fulwood Road
Sheffield S10 3BP
England

Typeset by Sheffield Academic Press
and
printed in Great Britain
by Billing & Sons Ltd
Worcester

British Library Cataloguing in Publication Data

Davis, Ellen F.
    Swallowing the scroll: textuality and the dynamics of discourse
    in Ezekiel's prophecy.
    1. Bible O.T. Ezekiel—Critical studies
    I. Title  II. Series  III. Series
    224'.406

    ISSN 0260-4493
    ISSN 0309-0787

    ISBN 1-85075-206-0

# CONTENTS

# PREFACE

The present work, a slightly revised version of my doctoral dissertation, received its first impetus from a conjunction of Yale University seminars offered in Spring 1985; and I am grateful to Brevard Childs, the late Hans Frei, and Cyrus Hamlin for encouraging the experiment. Robert Wilson was consistently helpful with his interest and questions, prodding me to consider the circumstances of writing as well as the text. For aid in identifying and obtaining research materials, I thank Ora Lipschitz of Jerusalem and the staff of Sterling Memorial Library; their graciousness made the work of research efficient and pleasurable far beyond my hopes. Yale University gave generous financial assistance; and the steady support, both financial and personal, of the Episcopal Church Foundation was a very great gift. Special thanks are due to Mary and Thomas Cushman for reminding me, week by week, that the project mattered, and why. First and last, I am deeply grateful to Brevard Childs for his wisdom in guiding me and his patience as I wandered my own way. In trusting me, he has taught me much.

This book is dedicated to three people who have nurtured and challenged me as parents and accompanied me as friends.

Works whose general argument is important for this study are included in the bibliography and cited by short notes in the text. Full notes are provided where only a particular point of reference is relevant. Because some of those kind enough to have taken an interest in this study do not read Hebrew, I have translated the biblical text wherever it was possible to do so without introducing a new difficulty. Extensive quotations from German and French works are also translated. All translations are my own unless otherwise noted.

# ABBREVIATIONS

| | |
|---|---|
| *ASTI* | *Annual of the Swedish Theological Institute* |
| ATANT | Abhandlungen zur Theologie des Alten und Neuen Testaments |
| BETL | Bibliotheca Ephemeridum Theologicarum Lovaniensium |
| BHS | Biblia Hebraica Stuttgartensia |
| BKAT | Biblischer Kommentar altes Testament |
| BT | Babylonian Talmud |
| BWAT | Beiträge zur Wissenschaft vom Alten Testament |
| BZAW | Beihefte zur Zeitschrift für die alttestamentliche Wissenschaft |
| *CBQ* | *Catholic Biblical Quarterly* |
| FS | Festschrift |
| HAT | Handbuch zum Alten Testament |
| *HTR* | *Harvard Theological Review* |
| *HUCA* | *Hebrew Union College Annual* |
| ICC | International Critical Commentary |
| *IEJ* | *Israel Exploration Journal* |
| *JAOS* | *Journal of the American Oriental Society* |
| *JBL* | *Journal of Biblical Literature* |
| JPS | Jewish Publication Society *Tanakh* |
| *JSOT* | *Journal for the Study of the Old Testament* |
| *JSS* | *Journal of Semitic Studies* |
| *NLH* | *New Literary History* |
| OTL | Old Testament Library |
| *RB* | *Revue Biblique* |
| SBL | Society of Biblical Literature |
| *VT* | *Vetus Testamentum* |
| VTSup | Vetus Testamentum, Supplements |
| *ZNW* | *Zeitschrift für die neutestamentliche Wissenschaft* |

For Frances, John, and Sister Mary Kathleen, S.L.G.

Chapter 1

FRAMING THE LITERARY QUESTION

... report me and my cause aright
To the unsatisfied (*Hamlet*, V, 2).

*History of the Problem*

'Architectonic' seems to be the scholarly epithet peculiar to the book
of Ezekiel. The primary object of critical research has been to
account for the book's salient feature: its comprehensive design,
which appears highly deliberate and distinguishes this work from
earlier collections of prophetic speeches. At the grossest level, there is
a discernible pattern in the thematic organization of the book, which
seems to divide quite sharply into three units: chs. 1-24, pronouncements of Jerusalem's doom; 25-32, oracles concerning the foreign
nations; 33-48, promises and visions of Israel's restoration. But
equally, there is an overall coherence of style and perspective,
maintained by the first-person narrative frame which anchors the
divine speeches. The book's comprehensive unity is evidenced also at
the level of content. Especially significant in this regard is the
sequence of three divine visions (1.1-3.15; 8.1-11.25; 40.1-48.35).[1]
The divine visions show the point of orientation for the prophet's
message: the divine presence (כבוד יי), which appears first in
connection with Ezekiel's call; next, in departure from the defiled
Temple, thereby both imaging the abandonment to disaster and
showing its just grounds; and finally, in reinvestiture of the new
Temple and the holy city. Thus one central image serves the
threefold function of prophetic validation, theodicy, and promise.

The impression of essential unity created by this structure long
delayed attempts at diachronic analysis of the sort which had been

applied to other prophetic books. The view that the book derives in its present form directly from the hand of the prophet prevailed through the first quarter of this century. Smend (1880) established the opinion that the work constitutes a literary unit:

> Most probably, therefore, the entire book was written down at a single stretch and the date of 40.1 may be considered as its approximate time of composition; the appendix in 29.17 ff., falling two years later, already presupposes its publication. As for the rest, Ezekiel wrote it during the siege of Tyre (cf. chs. 26ff.).[2]

Cornill (1886) took more seriously than Smend inconsistencies such as the supercession of the Tyre oracle and the absence of messianic references in chs. 40–48 (contrast 17.22-24; 21.32; 39.23-24, etc.) Accordingly, he saw in the book, not a whole plus a small appendix, but a more complex composition, evidencing several stages of development. Kraetzschmar (1900) used the technique of source criticism in an attempt to show the existence of two parallel recensions (representing first- and third-person perspectives) of an *Urtext*. Although the idea was not widely received, it was significant as a systematic treatment of tensions in the book which suggest extensive reworking as well as the influence of multiple writers or editors. While Herrmann (1908, 1924) set aside the notion of separate sources, he did draw a definite distinction between the prophet's original preaching and the editorial work (much, although not all of it, the prophet's own) which issued in the present form of the text. According to Herrmann's conception, what we have of Ezekiel's prophecy is not so much a unified composition as it is an anthology of individual pronouncements. The difference between the production of this work and that posited for earlier prophecy lies in the degree of the prophet's involvement in the literary process itself—i.e., in the phase which followed oral delivery of the oracles. Ezekiel is, therefore, conceived in the first instance as an orator and in the second as an editor, but never really as an author.[3]

Yet, despite increasing recognition of the tensions and complexity of the book, the scholarly consensus in the first part of the century was so little disturbed that S.R. Driver could affirm: 'No critical question arises in connexion with the authorship of the book, the whole from beginning to end bearing the stamp of a single mind'.[4]

Within a few years, however, consensus had yielded to hot debate. The work of Hölscher (1914-24) presented the first major challenge to the idea that the book as we have it derives essentially from the prophet himself.[5] It was his contention that one could account for the 'uncanny diversity' of elements only by seeing the book as coming from two worlds: that of the genuine Ezekiel and that of the redactors. He made it his object, then, to identify the principles which would permit their differentiation. Of these, the most important was a stylistic criterion. The genuine prophecies, according to Hölscher, derive from ecstatic experience and are recognizable for their 'dazzling, fantasy-filled and passionate rhetoric'.[6] In other words, Ezekiel was a poet, and his vivid utterances are, if not in all cases fully recoverable (due to extensive redactional revision), yet clearly distinct from the stiff, priestly prose which has accrued to them.

Hölscher's treatment has proven more stimulating than convincing. While he succeeded in exploding the assumption of the book's unity, Hölscher's view that little more than ten per cent of the book could be taken as genuine (144 of 1,273 verses, and some of those only in part) is too extreme for most critics.[7] Furthermore, he failed not only to show the basis for his principle that inspired utterance was exclusively formulated as poetry (begging the question of how that term is to be defined), but also to apply that principle consistently; at numerous points, the distinction between poetry and prose, as corresponding to prophetic and redactional material respectively, breaks down. For example, Hölscher assigns the poem in 32.1-16 to a redactor and, on the other hand, accepts as original the prose vision in 8.1–11.25.

Starting with this point of variant style, the book's peculiarities were acknowledged to be critical problems, and attempts to solve them—i.e., to bring the book into line with what was commonly thought about Israelite prophecy—proliferated. An issue which received particular attention was the prophet's geographical location. The question did not arise for the first time as a result of historical criticism. In the medieval period, Rashi had suggested that Ezekiel's prophetic career began before his deportation from Judah. His suggestion may well have been prompted by a desire to mitigate what was, from a rabbinic perspective, the scandal of revelation outside the land of Israel.[8] But in the modern context, the problem has been understood more in logical than in theological terms: if Ezekiel was first called to prophesy to the exiles, how does he show such minute

awareness of the situation in Jerusalam, even to the point of
addressing himself directly to the Jerusalemites and witnessing their
abominations in the Temple? Herntrich (1933) proposed that Ezekiel
worked in Jerusalem up until the time of its fall and credited an exilic
editor with the notion that the revelation was directed to him in
Babylon. Bertholet (1936) offered a widely received compromise
theory that Ezekiel had been called to prophesy twice, first in
Jerusalem and later in Babylon. He found evidence for this in the
complex call narrative, which he saw as a conflation of two different
experiences, one dominated by the chariot-throne vision, the other
by the swallowing of the scroll. Further complications were
introduced by Fischer[9] and Pfeiffer,[10] who suggested that Ezekiel
began prophesying in Babylon, then returned to Jerusalem, and
finally went back again into exile. The theory which posited maximal
mobility was advanced by Brownlee (1983), who saw in each locale
mentioned with the formula שׂים פָּנֶיךָ אֶל ('set your face toward. . .')
an indication of the prophet's peregrinations. The suggestion is
useful precisely by virtue of its implausibility. By extending as far as
possible the notion that wherever the prophet directs attention, there
he must be present in person, it shows the ascendancy of literalistic
zeal over literary sense to be a Pyrrhic victory.

   If the book's geographical ambivalence has been explained by
some in historical terms, others have reckoned it a fiction. The best-
publicized theory, as well as the most extreme, was that of Torrey
(1930), who maintained that the book was a pseudonymous creation
of the Hellenistic period (c. 230 BCE). The original form was a sort of
historical novel, set in Judah during Manasseh's reign; later (c. 200),
the text was reworked and the Babylonian setting created by a writer
from the school of the Chronicler.[11] A related proposal was that
offered by James Smith (1931), who, taking 'house of Israel' as a
political designation, saw Ezekiel as a prophet to the Northern
Israelites, active in Palestine and the diaspora after the fall of
Samaria. Smith considered the prophecy itself genuine, but the
Babylonian setting to be the fiction of a later redactor, who refocused
the text 'through Jewish eyes'.[12]

   With Torrey's work, the estimation of Ezekiel as a genuine prophet
reached its lowest ebb. Two decades later, Fohrer (1952-55) reasserted
the book's own claims regarding its origin and authority. He
returned to a conservative position, ascribing the basic structure in

its entirety to the prophet in Babylon, although finding throughout signs of later editing at other hands. Probably the least convincing aspect of his treatment was the attempt to establish a regular strophic pattern of short verses (two to three stresses). However, he succeeded in renewing confidence in the book's essential literary and historical integrity. Since Fohrer, the trend in scholarship has been to examine the text first as a linguistic object originating, according to its own claims, in the work of the sixth-century prophet, rather than to try moving behind the text in order to reconstruct its hidden background.[13]

In the last twenty years, Ezekiel research has become one of the most exciting and rapidly advancing areas of prophetic scholarship. The impetus has been provided largely by the publication of major commentaries by Zimmerli (1969) and Greenberg (1983; still in progress). Both adopt approaches which may be described as literary, although the sense in which the term applies is very different in each case, as the following discussion will demonstrate.

Zimmerli's work is characterized by a dual focus: first, reconstructing a posited basic form of the prophecy and tracing its subsequent elaboration to the present text; and second, analyzing literary forms and figures from form-critical and traditio-historical perspectives. He seeks to move beyond the impasse in which it seemed impossible fully to account for the heterogeneity which is evident even within the book's overall coherence, and at the same time to honor the claim of the first-person narrative, which credits the sixth-century prophet with the whole. Zimmerli accepts that the book comes in its basic form from Ezekiel in Babylon, but reckons further with a process of *Fortschreibung*, whereby a 'kernel element' underwent development, sometimes in several stages, either through the creation of additions following upon the basic theme (e.g., 16.44-58 and 59-63 are seen as two later strata to the original oracle, vv. 1-44), or through reworking of existing texts in order to reflect later events (e.g. 12.1-16, where the previously written material is adapted in light of the circumstances of Zedekiah's deportation). Certainly Zimmerli has made an important contribution toward answering those (Hölscher, Torrey, Irwin) who see no essential continuity—rather, see rupture, distortion, even falsification—between the original text (construed either as the prophet's own work or as a fiction) and later redactions. But, if Zimmerli has advanced our understanding of this material, his treatment is nevertheless flawed by the failure to pose certain questions concerning the implications of his own method.

The chief weakness of Zimmerli's commentary is his persistent recourse to form critical method without asking whether the context which he posits for Ezekiel's work is susceptible to illumination by that method. The goal of his analysis is to isolate the self-contained speeches which he assumes to lie at the base of the present text. Yet it is telling that Zimmerli cannot answer the form critic's fundamental question about how these speeches functioned in their original oral settings. Instead of trying to coordinate the speech forms with social practice in classical form critical manner, he traces their development through a purely literary process. Zimmerli is concerned only with identifying a compositional setting, which he calls 'the school of the prophet', where these supposedly simple speeches grew into their present complex forms. An index of the change which has taken place in the application of form critical categories is provided by his comment on the two-stage amplification of ch. 16:

> To the question about the setting in life of this process we must note that here we no longer have the free oracle, proclaimed publicly, as in earlier prophecy, but rather a kind of school treatment of preaching material which had already undergone a literary fixation.[14]

Similarly, his discussion of the recurrent 'recognition formula' (וידעתם/וידעו כי אני יי, 'And you/they shall know that I am YHWH') shows a disintegration of the method. He analyzes the formula as consisting of two parts, each with a different setting in life. The verbal 'assertion of recognition' is derived from 'the sphere of legal examination in which a sign of truth was demanded'; the object clause demonstrates 'the form of self-revelation of a person in his name'.[15] It is hard to see that Zimmerli has gained anything by the adduction of form critical categories; for the notion of legal examination does little to illumine Ezekiel's use of the formula in widely varying contexts and, further, he fails to show that self-introduction may properly be considered a *Gattung* to which certain formulaic language, fixed by repeated public usage, belongs. Rather than anchoring the prophet's language in the forms of community life, Zimmerli argues for its place in Ezekiel's overall rhetorical and theological purpose.[16] While I concur that this is the most fruitful approach for exegesis, it should be acknowledged as a departure from the assumptions and concerns central to form criticism, and the conditions necessitating that departure should be explored.

A related problem is the fact that, while Zimmerli does not admit a discontinuity between the basic text and the editorial additions, he posits one which is even more fundamental, for it lies within the sphere of the prophet's own activity. For Zimmerli, it is crucial to distinguish, temporally and also in qualitative terms, between the 'real core of prophetic experience', associated with the period of Ezekiel's preaching activity, and a subsequent process of 'graphic meditation' in an academic setting, emanating in the present text.[17] The basis of this distinction would seem to be a view of the prophetic function compatible with form criticism: viz., that the prophet is a spontaneous orator who uses the simple speech forms of an oral culture to frame divine oracles.

Yet Zimmerli fails to take fully into account the change in the prophetic role which occurs with Ezekiel, even though the occurrence of such a change is implicit in his critical methodology. His notion of *Fortschreibung* entails a recognition that Ezekiel, more than any earlier prophet, was involved in activity best described as pedagogical, even scholarly:

> That the prophet himself knew something of school instruction, which is phenomenologically very different from the older prophetic preaching in public, is made very clear by passages such as chs. 18, 33.1-9, 10-20. Thus besides the oral proclamation of rhythmically composed sayings, which continued the manner of preaching of earlier prophets, we must reckon that the prophet himself undertook the secondary work of learned commentary upon and further elaboration of his prophecies, i.e., with a kind of 'school activity'.[18]

It is questionable whether this phase can be fully separated from the original prophetic communication, as Zimmerli tries to do. Indeed, the very thing for which we lack evidence is the fundamental stratum of orally conceived preaching, which should presumably consist of relatively simple units resembling those found in eighth-century prophecy. Although Zimmerli does not succeed in finding the speech forms of classical prophecy, he does locate 'the unaltered deposit of spoken address' in passages which display a regular rhythm, either in poetry (e.g. the lament meter of chs. 19 and 26.15-18) or in 'elevated prose' (chs. 16 and 23). 'Rhythm is for the ear, and not for the eye and the reflective spirit'.[19]

Yet the presence of rhythm (and I agree that there are some passages in which at least an approximate rhythm can be found) does not, as Zimmerli suggests, prove that a given piece is an oral composition. What he does not take into account is the possibility that the spoken word of the prophet was *itself* a literary work, i.e., that it was composed in writing, although intended for oral delivery. Zimmerli seems to be hampered by the idea, common in biblical scholarship since Gunkel's revolutionary work opened up the long phase of oral development lying behind the biblical text, that oral compositions are somehow more genuine than written ones. He is anxious to guard Ezekiel against the charge (especially with respect to the visions and the symbolic acts) of being a writer, in the sense of one who creates 'pure literary fiction'. But to say that these accounts are fundamentally literary in their formulation is not the same as seeing them as unfounded in actual experience.

The work of Widengren (1948) and Lindblom (1962) is useful in showing the relation between revelatory experience and literary production as the primary mode of expression. Lindblom considers chs. 40–48 to comprise mostly visions of the literary or 'fictitious' sort, produced in an exalted but not genuinely ecstatic state of mind: 'After the passing of the ecstatic rapture the prophet worked out all the details contained in the nine chapters, giving to all that emerged in his imagination and reflection the form of a long series of visionary experiences linked to the basic ecstatic visions'.[20] But Lindblom does not really develop the significance of this sort of sustained reflection with respect to the role which writing had come to play in prophecy. He regards the book as a collection of originally independent oracles analogous to Isaiah, Jeremiah, etc. Yet Lindblom acknowledges that 'collections of the first order', such as are found in these other books, are missing in Ezekiel; there seems to have been only one chief collector of the oracles. It is odd, then, that he never considers the possibility that this collector might have been Ezekiel himself, nor does he explain how another editor could have created such a strong impression of unity from a large number of independent oracles.

Widengren grants a much more important place to writing, not only in Ezekiel's activity, but within Israelite religious tradition as a whole: 'The process of recording, collecting, and preserving the master's words and actions. . . is from the outset bound up with the process of committing the traditions to paper'.[21] He draws upon the work of T. Andrae[22] to determine the relation between prophetic experience and literary form. Like Lindblom, he distinguishes two types of vision, primarily on the basis of the amount of detail recorded: one, 'the clear, plastic one with sharp outlines' and the other, the complex sort exemplified by Ezekiel's inaugural vision, which has a tendency toward abstruseness, even visual absurdity, and often serves a symbolical or moralizing function. Concerning the latter type, he comments:

> Andrae concludes that, from a psychological point of view, there must be a rather considerable distance between the original experience and its reflecting in the committing to paper. Everything points in the direction of the accompanying verbal inspiration's being to a rather great extent a result of the writer's own conscious efforts.[23]

Two observations are relevant to the comments already made about Zimmerli's approach. First, neither Widengren nor Andrae casts any doubt upon the reality of the experience which thus achieves literary expression. Second, there is no indication that this kind of expression follows upon and elaborates an oral communication. The crucial point, which will be developed further in this essay, is that writing, even in the ancient world, did not serve only as a way of preserving and amplifying oral material or, alternately, of creating fictions out of whole cloth. Writing may also be a way of ordering experience and rendering it communicable in the first instance; and, further, it facilitates a complexity of interaction between speaker and addressee which might otherwise be impossible. Zimmerli's almost exclusive attention to the *sources* of language (from form critical and traditio-historical perspectives) should be supplemented by consideration of a problem which is perhaps even more important in determining Ezekiel's place among the prophets: namely, what *function* is served by the book's distinctive forms of speech?

Greenberg's approach differs radically from Zimmerli's in both its presuppositions and its goal. Greenberg for the most part avoids diachronic analysis, although he sometimes grants the possibility that a section represents a final rather than an original unity.[24] His perspective is essentially aesthetic; Greenberg looks for recurrent themes and large patterns which show the book as a whole to be 'the product of art and intelligent design'.[25] Moreover, the breadth and coherence of the design is emphasized by his decision to view the text synchronically. He describes his method thus: 'Our holistic method seeks to reconstitute the perception of the text by an ideal reader living at a time when it had reached its present disposition. "Ideal reader" is a personified realization of the possibilities inherent in the text at that moment'.[26]

This approach is not a naïve embracing of precritical assumptions (of a sort which are applied without discrimination to most or all biblical books) about authorial unity. Nor does it represent, regardless of Greenberg's use of terminology derived from contemporary literary criticism, a post-modern decision to read ahistorically, even aggressively against the original meaning of the text and the intention of its creator(s), in order to establish the reader's perspective as sovereign. Rather, the contention that it is valid to treat this particular book from a synchronic perspective rests upon a critical judgment about its compositional character. A chief aim of Greenberg's commentary is to illustrate and awaken appreciation for the style of the prophet, as well as to show that its complexity is consistent both with Ezekiel's rhetorical purpose and with the literary conventions of the ancient world. His working assumption is that the present form of the text expresses a consistent trend of thought proceeding from

> an individual mind of powerful and passionate proclivities. The chronology of the oracles and the historical circumstances reflected in them assign them to a narrow range well within the span of a single life. The persuasion grows on one as piece after piece falls into the established patterns and ideas that a coherent world of vision is emerging, contemporary with the sixth-century prophet and decisively shaped by him, if not the very words of Ezekiel himself.[27]

Greenberg's commentary is unquestionably valuable for the challenge it offers to preconceptions bred of the unreflective application of historical critical method: especially, the idea that genuine prophecy should not display the variety of stylistic features and the breadth of artistic conception found in the kind of deliberate creation we normally call 'literature'. However, while his skillful readings often illumine the way the text creates its effects and may well reflect authorial or editorial intentions, I think his general avoidance of the question of diachronic development misses an important aspect of how the linguistic possibilities inherent in a text may be recognized and exploited, thereby enriching over a period of time the author's original work. Greenberg's occasional nod to a 'gloss'[28] does not really do justice to the process of progressive interpretation which seems to have contributed to the final shape of this book.

From the standpoint of the present study, however, the more serious problem with Greenberg's work is his failure to treat what would seem to be one of the most interesting questions to which his treatment gives rise. Certainly he acknowledges the exquisite patterning which he discerns to be that of a distinctively literary creation. Yet it is curious that Greenberg does not bring the implications of this fact to bear upon a consideration of the role of the prophet. He never asks what kind of prophet, *qua* prophet, would produce such discourse, or what kind of audience could apprehend it.

In general, while Greenberg continually holds forth the possibility that the literary mind responsible for shaping the text is Ezekiel's, he avoids references to the prophet as a writer. This appears most clearly from the methodological statement which appeared several years before the first volume of the commentary, where he expresses his hope 'to experience the editor–canonizer as a fellow–intelligence'.[29] Whether or not this 'editor–canonizer' is identified with Ezekiel himself (and the overall tenor of Greenberg's work would seem to support this identification), the term raises difficult historical questions which Greenberg does not attempt to answer. An important question, but one which leads too far afield to warrant attention here, is whether the term 'canonizer' is really appropriate in this period.[30] However, I assume that what Greenberg means is the person responsible for production of the final form of the text. He would, then, keep the time frame for the transcription and final editing of this prophecy within the span conceivable for Ezekiel's own activity. But even if this point be granted, at least with respect to the major development of the book, what needs to be pressed is inquiry into the conditions and processes which have resulted in consolidation of the tradition of this prophet within such a short period of time.

Among recent studies whose approach to the book is, broadly speaking, literary, the exegetical work of Fishbane and Talmon (singly and in collaboration) should be noted. On particular passages, it may be usefully compared with Zimmerli's and Greenberg's more extensive treatments, with which it has affinities on either side, while avoiding certain pitfalls of their methods. Fishbane and Talmon characterize Ezekiel as a 'compiler–composer' (מחבר-מסדר).[31] In attempting to identify the principles of composition which he employed, they offer a structural analysis more refined than Zimmerli's attempt to separate chronological strata on a form-critical basis. On the other hand, they operate with a more flexible time frame than does Greenberg, allowing for Ezekiel's incorporation of earlier material (e.g. a Temple blueprint) and also for later changes at the hands of his students:

> Woe to that book if it had not been so! Change in books and growth in books are testimony to their vital existence... Concerning the books of the prophets, the teachers of their contemporaries, certainly the process was such. It is reasonable to think, and almost has the force of certainty, that at the beginning they did not record sayings in writing but passed them on orally. And as for the sayings of the prophets, certainly they were passed on orally by more than one student. The fact that the prophet 'bound' his teaching upon his students does not mean that he bound a single teaching only. Clearly, every hearer would interpret and every hearer would alter.[32] And everyone who passed on the sayings which he heard, he also would interpret, supplement, and elucidate.[33]

These remarks are especially interesting with respect to the question of the changes which the book underwent in the process of transmission, for Talmon believes that the collection of Ezekiel's speeches and 'essays' (מסותיו) assumed written form under the prophet's own hand.[34] It is important to realize, however, that in a society whose pedagogical and communications systems still place primary emphasis on memorization and oral transmission (out of necessity as much as principle, for manuscripts are always scarce and delicate), material is unlikely to be frozen in the form in which it is first inscribed. Moreover, there are indications that well into the rabbinic period, the concept of authorship was not a precise or exclusive one;[35] so there is no reason to think that in the sixth century, Ezekiel's disciples would have scrupled about making unsigned additions to their master's words. Rather, such amplifications and clarifications attest to the high regard in which the text was held.

It is the common failing of all modern studies, even those which consider the text to be essentially the creation of a single mind, that they do not treat the functional aspects of Ezekiel's status as a writer. There is no inquiry into how this new mode of prophetic activity might correspond to changing social circumstances, in what way the shift to writing represents an attempt to deal with new problems faced by the first prophet of the exile and sets new conditions for the reception of the prophet and his message by the community. In order to find any serious consideration of these points, it is necessary to turn back to the early period of critical scholarship.

In 1841, Ewald identified this book as representing a new species of literature, one which reflects 'the remodelling of prophetic thought and style' in accordance with the situation of a writer.[36] Although he considers that the dumbness expresses the 'solitary prophetic meditation and thought' which absorbed Ezekiel from the time of his call, Ewald does not completely deny him any speaking activity: most of the book was written after the fall of the city, when Ezekiel's public activities were presumably more closely circumscribed. While the connection between the larger social situation and the 'literary leisure' from which the book emerged is not tightly drawn, it is to Ewald's credit that he recognizes factors such as dispersion, foreign domination, and the dissolution of the nation's decision-making apparatus as having an effect upon the style of prophecy. Further, he perceives a change in rhetorical purpose, with various artistic forms designed to stimulate the imagination (histories, elaborated visions, and symbolic narratives) increasingly replacing direct challenges to action. While regretting the change whereby 'the author distinguishes himself at the expense of the prophet',[37] Ewald also notes the enlarged capacity of these speech forms, as compared to those of earlier prophecy. As a writer, Ezekiel has more scope for learned discourse on matters of priestly Torah, the mythological structures of the pagan nations, depictions of the earthly sanctuary; he can take up topics never previously treated by Israel's prophets, such as those in chs. 40–48. Ewald's evaluation of this new trend in prophecy is finally a positive one. Because of its distinctive qualities—orderliness, precision and copiousness of expression—

> writing became a spiritual renewal and fresh creation of oral discourse, a creation which, though it would certainly have been impossible unless the language of public speech had preceded it

with its life and effectiveness, yet in many respects surpasses this, excelling it by virtue of its own peculiar purposes and advantages.[38]

Orelli (1896) also considers the constraints imposed by exile to have had a determinative effect on the form assumed by Ezekiel's prophecy. He is careful to designate Ezekiel's position as a liminal one, marking what is new without making a complete separation from the old style of prophecy. Like Ewald, he maintains that Ezekiel, while living in a condition of enforced tranquillity, to which corresponds 'the contemplative character of his prophetic Muse', also delivered speeches aloud, and that it is mistaken to make of him a mere writer. He continues:

> On the other hand, it is correct that the written record was of particular importance for him, especially since his speeches could otherwise benefit only the smallest portion of his people and the content itself called for a painstaking inscription.[39]

Orelli notes also the stylistic change which accompanies this new form of prophetic expression, evident especially in the exhaustive detail with which Ezekiel sets forth his visions. His distinctiveness is conspicuous already in the call narrative. Whereas Isaiah's heavenly vision (ch. 6), sketched with a few bold strokes, has the force of an immediate impression, Ezekiel's laborious style attests that the prophet is reflecting on his experience from a distance, as well as devoting considerable time to its exposition. A particularly interesting aspect of Orelli's discussion is the observation that this mode of prophecy, laden with detail and rapidly changing images, also places new demands on the attention of those for whom Ezekiel spoke or wrote. In other words, the move to writing changes not only the role of the prophet, but also that of the audience, who must themselves become more patient listeners and conscientious interpreters of the prophetic word.

### Outlining a Functional Approach

No one in this century has followed the direction pointed by Ewald and Orelli in exploring the connection between the prophet's social circumstances and the literary style of his prophecy. With the erosion—or better, in view of the impact of Hölscher's work, the explosion—of the early critical consensus about the book's substantial unity, the insight about its distinctive speech forms having arisen *as a function of writing* seems to have receded into the background of the discussion. It is this insight which I aim to develop, employing some of the tools provided by contemporary studies in the pragmatics of written discourse and literary language. The question to be pursued is a functional one: what factors operative in Ezekiel's environment constitute a new kind of challenge to the prophet in communicating his message, and how does writing afford him the linguistic means to answer that challenge? My goal is to find a way of accounting for the elements in this book which violate our preconceptions about prophetic speech (as, perhaps, they violated those of Ezekiel's contemporaries), while yet taking seriously his own claim to stand in the line of Israel's prophets.

It will be evident that, despite my criticisms of their approaches, I am much indebted to Zimmerli and Greenberg for their contributions to an understanding of the process by which the present text may have evolved and the dynamics whereby it achieves its effects as a coherent—if not smooth—piece of literature. The present study would have been impossible without the efforts and accomplishments of these two scholars, and I maintain them throughout as my most important dialogue partners. In some contrast, however, to their (respectively) historical and holistic literary treatments, here particular attention is given to aspects of Ezekiel's speech which reveal a new dynamics of prophetic discourse. In other words, I am concerned with how, working under the conditions of the exile, Ezekiel is engaged in remodelling prophecy as a form of social interaction.

There is an affinity between the method I propose to develop here and a basic premise of form criticism: namely, that some correlation can and should be drawn between sociological data and formal literary analysis. Nonetheless, by formulating the literary question in a functional way, I hope to treat aspects of linguistic *usage* in a given historical situation which are overlooked by form critical inquiry into the historical *sources* of linguistic forms. The next chapter will outline the basic elements of a theory of written discourse with an aim to show what special opportunities and constraints are introduced into the communications situation with the shift from live to written speech. This theoretical material forms the background for an investigation of textual properties in relation to the social circumstances in which this prophecy was promulgated.

Throughout the study, I attempt to keep uppermost a concern for what might be called the 'appropriateness conditions' of Ezekiel's distinctive style.[40] Contemporary literary analyses of biblical texts have sometimes shown too little regard for the fact that discourse emerges through the interplay of a speaker's or author's intentions and the expectations of those addressed in an environment formed by certain linguistic conventions and modes of communication. There is a danger that the results of such analyses may reflect more the literary sensibilities of modern interpreters (nurtured on an individual reader's leisurely perusal of private copies of texts which come from the desk of a single author/editor) than any compositional notion which an ancient writer might have had. Proper assessment of Ezekiel's achievement requires a sociologically informed awareness of the differences between his culture and our own with respect to the interaction of oral speech and literary activity.

This investigation is guided by the following presuppositions and principles:

1. While significant diachronic change in the text is at many points probable, a strong reading should render the text synchronically intelligible at every stage of development. That is, while a passage may have been elaborated in such a way as to enhance or to alter its earlier meaning, thereby perhaps introducing ambiguities and tensions, nonetheless it is assumed that the general intention and effect of these changes was to produce a meaningful text. Therefore, 'explanations' which cite redactional activity and yet offer no positive understanding of the current shape of the text are avoided.

2. Ezekiel's words and actions are to be understood as elements of his public activity as a prophet, or as literary representations of such activity. Accordingly, attempts to account for them purely in terms of pathological phenomena or other peculiarities of the prophet's personality are excluded.

3. Indications given by the text regarding the circumstances of its composition are of primary significance. These include the first-person narrative frame, the Babylonian setting and the dates for Ezekiel's activity, and the consistent theocentric emphasis.

4. Complex manipulation of language is assumed to be a

feature of Ezekiel's own work, although not in all cases to reflect a single stage of his composition. On this assumption, the search for discrete forms resembling those of classical Israelite prophecy must be supplemented by a broader appreciation of literary patterning and also by an awareness of the formal and functional distinctiveness of written speech—the inference being, of course, that Ezekiel was not a linguistic theorist but rather a highly competent user of language.

The fact that it is often hazardous and in many cases impossible to determine at what stage of transmission and through whose hands particular material has entered the text is obviously pertinent to a literary investigation. My arguments are generally based on features of the text which are acknowledged by all but the most extreme critics to be Ezekiel's own; wherever attribution is seriously debated, I note the relation of my argument to that debate.

Finally, something must be said about the extremely problematic state of the book's textual transmission. I do not pretend to have wrestled with many of these problems or solved any of them. The chief issue, however, is whether such a degree of textual obscurity, inconsistency, and uncertainty is compatible with my claim that Ezekiel's prophecy was actually conceived in writing. I maintain that it is, that, indeed, written composition may actually have contributed to some of the difficulties of the text. There is a frequent awkwardness of style which must be considered an original element, possibly resulting from Ezekiel's experimentation with new speech forms and his own pioneering role as a writer–prophet. The confusing alternation of seond- and third-person speech in the denunciation of the corrupt prophets (13.2-16) may be cited as an example of a 'text critical' problem which is best considered in terms of Ezekiel's liminality.[41] In the absence of a literary convention governing this kind of 'fictitious speech',[42] the prophet's disposition vacillates between that of the orator and that of the writer, respectively engaged in direct confrontation and exposition.

The evolution of style in every literature bears the marks of trial and error—or at least, of greater and lesser successes. William Chase Greene comments instructively on the difference between the clumsiness of Herodotus' historiographic prose and the far more polished structure of Homer's epics: 'The spoken word had found its perfect form just as it was being reduced to writing; the written word, seeking to "answer questions," is still groping for appropriate form'.[43] A number of the obscure features of Ezekiel's prophecy assume functional significance when examined as attempts to find a new literary idiom for prophecy. Critics therefore do well to be wary of excising material as secondary simply because it does not demonstrate consistently felicitous style or conform neatly to models familiar from classical prophetic literature.

It is probable also that difficulties were subsequently introduced by tradents baffled by the degree of lexical and syntactical complexity and the unprecedented variety of forms which this material displays. Moreover, there is no reason to suppose that they inherited a uniform text tradition from the prophet.[44] The idea that writers always produce only one final version of their work derives more from the exigencies of commercial publication than from the habits of writers themselves. Famous counter-examples within the modern period include the two or three authorized versions of Wordsworth's *The Prelude*, or Byron's *The Giaour*, of which we have many pre-publication and published forms, varying widely in length and substance, as well as in such minor features as punctuation and capitalization.[45] It is quite possible that the mode in which Ezekiel worked actually multiplied the opportunities for choice and therefore inevitably for confusion in transmitting the text tradition.

# Chapter 2

## PROPHECY IN TRANSITION

*nam.dub.sar.ra ama.gù.dé.ke₄.e.ne a.a.um.me.a.ke₄.eš*

The scribal art is the mother of orators and the father of scholars.[1]

The peculiarly detailed style of Ezekiel's visions is the basis of the Talmud's comparison between Ezekiel and Isaiah as resembling, respectively, a villager (בן כפר) and a townsman (בן כרך) who saw a king.[2] Rashi explains that the former, being completely unaccustomed to the sight, naturally gives his impressions in greater detail. But the Tosafists (the twelfth- and thirteenth-century scholars who composed additions—'tosafot'—to Rashi's commentary) see another point: namely, that because the villager's circumstances do not ordinarily admit of such an event, he has a greater challenge in convincing his hearers that he really did see the king. The actual difference to which the analogy points is not, of course, the relative sophistication of the two prophets (for Ezekiel was as much an urbanite as Isaiah), but the fact that Ezekiel's revelatory experience occurred in a situation in which such a thing was not thought to be possible: in exile, outside the land of Israel.

The remarks of the medieval commentators are particularly interesting, for they set forth two lines of interpretation which remain important alternatives in Ezekiel scholarship. With respect to the problem of accounting for the peculiar nature of the visions or, indeed, of the book as a whole, the first (Rashi's) suggests that the solution lies in whatever can be determined about Ezekiel's personal disposition. Most modern studies which share the same perspective evoke psychological phenomena or the particular interests and obsessions bred by the priesthood. But the second approach (the Tosafists') points in quite a different direction, suggesting that this style of prophecy may be a response to external circumstances which created difficulties for Ezekiel in establishing his message as authoritative. As the first prophet to receive a vision outside the land, he had to produce a fuller record in order to be believed. This approach, then, treats prophecy, not primarily in the context of private religious experience, but rather as an interactive social phenomenon whose form is adaptable to change in the context of discourse.

In the following chapters, I will try to show that this second line of inquiry, while generally less preferred by Ezekiel scholars, is the more fruitful. But the starting point for my investigation is not identical with that of the Tosafists. Their insight about the connection between the circumstances and the style of Ezekiel's prophecy was prompted by theological reflection on the apparent incongruity of visions of Israel's God and the Temple in Jerusalem being granted in exile. I intend to pursue the connection from another angle, focusing on the crucial and irreversible cultural shift whereby the religious life of Israel became increasingly oriented toward the production and interpretation of texts, a shift which in turn profoundly altered the prophet's social role. It is the purpose of this chapter to lay a theoretical foundation for understanding the nature of that shift.

### Orality and Writing: Language in Transition

There is no debate about the fact that the exilic community participated in extensive literary activity—arguably, the most significant in all Israel's history.[3] Although there must have existed before the fall some form of Scripture, probably comprising the basic elements of the Torah and much of the Prophets, the concentrated work of consolidation, revision, and new creation in which the exiles engaged seems to have been at least in part a way of meeting the greatest threat Israelite culture had faced. Ivan Engnell, consistent with the Scandinavian assertion of the primacy and superiority of the oral tradition, characterized the response as an indication of weakened faith in the spoken word and 'a general crisis of confidence'.[4] Ackroyd offers a more positive evaluation of written fixation of the tradition as 'an attempt at guaranteeing a continuity which might otherwise be lost'.[5]

Curiously, however, little attention has been paid to the fact that increased use of writing not only serves compensatory and preservative functions, but also carries an inherent creative potential. This blind spot among biblical scholars may be an indication of the extent to which Gunkel's observations about the oral foundations of Hebrew literature have prevailed and been generalized. Mendenhall expresses a view which is widely held: 'The writing down of traditions in the ancient world comes at the end of an era, not at its beginning. Writing is used to preserve, not, as in the modern scholarly world, to create.'[6]

The results of recent research in the history of language and its uses challenge this view. It has become increasingly evident that writing did play a creative role in shaping ancient cultures and, furthermore, that the gradual shift from a primarily oral society to one which makes frequent and varied usage of writing is far from superficial. There is, indeed, no technological development which has more profoundly affected human interaction.

Written communications are, relative to oral ones, both less situationally concrete and more internally specific. Oral speech depends for clarity of meaning on a multitude of non-verbal indicators such as the speaker's gestures, intonation, facial expression, mode of dress, props, and especially upon the historical experience and situational understanding common to the speaker and the audience. The meaning of living speech is considered, for all practical purposes, identical with the immediate intention of the speaker; to miss this meaning is generally judged to be negligent or perverse listening, not a creative act of interpretation. While the possibility of ambiguity and well-intentioned misunderstanding is never quite excluded, the dialogical situation minimizes this by affording the opportunity for questioning and challenge by the audience, for clarification and self-correction by the speaker.

In written language, however, the bond between 'speaker' and 'hearer' within a given set of historical circumstances is, if not broken, then at least greatly attenuated. Lacking such external supports, written speech must offer guides to meaning almost wholly within the verbal channel.[7] The tools which any written language devises to meet this exigency are a precise sign system and a set of lexical and syntactic conventions which provide a fairly high degree of semantic explicitness. But these technological advances do more than render inscribed discourse intelligible. They also give it a relation to the circumstances of its creation which differs from that of oral speech—a relation often characterized as autonomy. This means, first of all, that the meaning of written language is not wholly identifiable with the intention of its originator, who is not normally present with the text to support or explain its meaning. Autonomy means, furthermore, that the text is able to enter situations and to address readers unknown to its author. Often the fact that the text can escape or outlive the situation which gives it rise is precisely the reason for writing.

The ramifications of this capability are far-reaching indeed. Ricoeur contends that 'the emancipation of the text from the oral situation entails a veritable upheaval in the relations between language and the world, as well as in the relation between language and the various subjectivities involved'.[8] The phenomenon of writing reveals a new dialectic of discourse whose partners are, properly speaking, the text and its readers. There is, however, a measure of inequality to their partnership, for the text alone 'speaks'. Written discourse makes no allowance for retort, defence, or correction from its readers. Yet the text's voice can be heard only through the consent of its partners, which they grant through the act of reading. Such consent is finally more crucial for written discourse than for spoken; for the living voice reaches all those within earshot, whether or not they wish to hear, but the text has the opportunity of impressing only those who are willing to concede in advance the possibility of its being important and to make an investment of their attention.

The role of the audience constitutes an important qualification respecting the autonomous character of written language. Margaret Rader suggests that such autonomy 'is not so much a reality as it is a goal or a felt need on the part of those who must communicate with people from a wide variety of cultural backgrounds'.[9] Post-structuralist literary criticism and sociological studies of written discourse share a common emphasis on the literary process, in which the reader is an indispensable participant. Rader comments further:

> Writing, because of its well-known characteristic of being removed from an immediate conversational situation, is particularly well suited for a kind of language use which maximally depends on the contribution of background information on the part of the reader, even as it minimally depends on paralinguistic, postural, or gestural channels. This kind of language use tends toward syntactic complexity and lexical elaboration. . . to control and make possible the development of a complex image in the mind of the reader.[10]

Readers bring to bear on the text their own prior experience of the world and knowledge of literary conventions and in turn may allow its linguistic representations to inform and alter their conceptions. The precision of written discourse facilitates fuller exploitation of this process than is normally possible with spoken language: 'Only in writing can the inference-suggesting information be so carefully controlled and restricted even as inferring and imaging are given full rein'.[11]

This active involvement of the reader means, then, that the text is not finally autonomous. Its relative freedom from the intentions of its author and the circumstances of its origin is but the precondition whereby it becomes linked with other consciousnesses and embedded in new circumstances which provide the historical context—or, more accurately, a variety of such contexts—for its interpretation. Another aspect of the contextualization of written discourse is the fact that texts may participate in the 'quasi-world' of literature; they have the ability 'to enter into relation with all other texts, which come to take the place of the circumstantial reality referred to by living speech'.[12] That is to say, texts are read in the light of other texts, and this relation is both a source of their richness and a limitation on their autonomy.

There are indications that expanded use of writing affects other aspects of discourse and thought, not just at the level of the individual consciousness, or in the interchange between particular writers and readers, but throughout the cultural sphere. As a result of its greater inherent explicitness, and also its more luxurious relation to time (for both creation and assimilation), written language is less firmly bound to the common stock of ideas, stories, familiar phrases and patterns upon which oral speech largely depends for ready intelligibility to an audience and for manageability by a speaker or reciter. Familiarity is an important value in traditional story-telling, although the narrator's distinctive style—varying also to some extent with each performance—undoubtedly contributes to the interest.[13] The traditional oral performance may be construed as an instance of the community as a whole, all the generations through which the tale has evolved, addressing the present audience, with one individual serving as its mouthpiece.[14] But the move to writing entails emergence of an authorial consciousness, and with that a new possibility for the use of language. No longer restricted to recreating what everyone already knows, language acquires the capacity to serve as 'an exploratory device. . . an instrument for the formulation and preservation of original statements that [can] violate readers' expectancies and commonsense knowledge'.[15]

As is evident from the preceding remarks about the reader's role, the exploratory dimension of written language is not exhausted or exclusively controlled by the writer. Writing is always vulnerable to the possibility of meaning something more or other than what the author intended. Because a written piece perdures to be read and interpreted in a variety of circumstances which is theoretically unlimited, the act of inscription paradoxically both insures the preservation of speech and perpetuates debate about its meaning. Writing, moreover, elicits more writing; it invites amplification, exegesis, commentary. The loosening of the written text from a fixed frame of reference, its potential for addressing readers whose own frames of reference are incalculably diverse, and further, its interaction with other texts within a literary tradition upon which it draws and against which it reacts—these are the characteristics which create the possibility of multiple meanings and generate out of the inscription of discourse the dynamics of interpretation.

Havelock has presented an important argument concerning the exploratory and ultimately revolutionary capacity inherent in writing. He contends that Plato's work is directed toward harnessing the power of writing in an educational system based on *episteme* (scientific rationalism or rational analysis), in contrast to traditional rote learning according to *mimesis* ('the total act of poetic representation').[16] The animus which Plato evinces in excluding poets from educational activity in the Republic stems from his conviction that the poetic synthesis of experience is conducive only to reflexive thought and feeling, whereas he challenges his contemporaries to a more reflective response.

> He asks of men that instead they should examine this experience and rearrange it, that they should think about what they say, instead of just saying it. And they should separate themselves from it instead of identifying with it; they themselves should become the 'subject' who stands apart from the 'object' and reconsiders it and analyses it and evaluates it, instead of just 'imitating' it.[17]

Such a separation between the knower and the known is only possible, according to Havelock, through writing, which makes discourse visible and thereby sets a distance between the utterance and its originator.

Ricoeur notes that 'a primitive type of distanciation' is an element even of oral discourse, a function of the fact that all discourse is informed by an intentionality which endures beyond the fleeting language event itself.[18] But this feature is greatly enhanced by the inscription of discourse, whereby it is loosed from its moorings in circumstantial reality in the ways discussed above.

> The world of the text is therefore not the world of everyday language. In this sense, it constitutes a new sort of distanciation from the real itself. . . . Everyday reality is thereby metamorphised by what could be called the imaginative variations which literature carries out on the real.[19]

Ricoeur here refers specifically to imaginative literature, i.e., fiction and poetry. Yet his observation might well be applied to all literary language, whose every form is to some degree unnatural, a studied representation of reality which is comprehensible only to those familiar with its conventions.[20] And adaptation to life in that world of the text involves a fundamental reorientation. The implication of the study of written discourse as a distinct phenomenon is that, precisely by virtue of its status as the product of conscious effort, writing also becomes productive of an altered intellectual awareness. Because writing sets a distance not only between interlocutors but also between each individual and his or her own verbal acts, writing heightens consciousness of discourse, of both the act of expression and that of understanding. Because writing makes language visible, it promotes greater sensitivity to words[21] and their usage, to various possibilities for the flow of speech, to the range of semantic options and therefore to the whole question of 'meaning' at some remove from immediate circumstances.

The consequences are surely vast. Goody, Watt and Ong in particular have followed Havelock in making strong claims regarding the significance of writing for cultural and intellectual achievement. These include suggestions that differences usually conceived in terms of such dichotomies as savage/domesticated, pre-logical/logical, magical/scientific, can be more fruitfully considered in relation to the mechanics of communication, and further that the 'cumulative scepticism' which underlies a critical attitude toward received wisdom is a function of literate activity.[22] Yet one must be cautious of absolute claims. Certainly modern history offers sufficient tragic examples to refute the notion that highly literate societies are always correspondingly sceptical of social dogma. On the other hand, the early Israelites' massive reconceptualization of traditional beliefs and cultural institutions does not seem in the first instance to have resulted from the examination of texts. Literacy is better seen as an ingredient, not a recipe for various forms of critical thinking or social development. The way in which an individual or a society takes advantage of the opportunities that literacy affords reflects prior dispositions as well as interaction with a complex of political, economic, and other social factors.

Furthermore, orality and literacy are not strict alternatives but rather poles of a continuum, and each society—indeed, each literary work—must be individually assessed with respect to its location and the manner of its accommodation to either pole. Finnegan has been especially insistent that variations among literate or non-literate societies are as important as differences between the two categories; and she further asserts the existence of 'literature' (as, for example, evidencing concern for form and style, or showing the influence of individual composers) even in non-writing cultures.[23] Hirsch also notes that the functional distinction between discourse which is situationally concrete and that which is semantically exact does not coincide wholly with (respectively) oral and written media. He observes the contrast between elaborated and restricted linguistic codes, both employed in oral speech, but in different contexts. An elaborated code employs the explicit style generally associated with writing, evidencing both grammatical and lexical precision[24] in order to render the communication intelligible to a heterogeneous group, whose common experience with the speaker and each other cannot be assumed. A restricted code, on the other hand, is appropriate within a small homogeneous group whose shared frame of reference provides the context for its decipherment. Some speech genres are functionally aberrant: a radio talk, like writing, addresses an unknown audience and conveys meaning without benefit of the speaker's personal presence; a private note, on the other hand, often imitates the linguistic conventions of living speech.

Among various qualifications of the distinction between speaking and writing, the most important for the purposes of this study is the historical one. Literary style has had a long and, in most of its phases, slow evolution; and only in comparatively modern times has it moved far from conscious or unconscious imitation of oral speech forms. Ong stresses the persistence of oral characteristics in written expression:

> Only very gradually does writing become composition in writing, a kind of discourse—poetic or otherwise—that is put together without a feeling the one writing is actually speaking aloud (as early writers may well have done in composing). . . . Oral habits of thought and expression, including massive use of formulaic elements, sustained in use largely by the teaching of the old classical rhetoric, still marked prose style of almost every sort in Tudor England some two thousand years after Plato's campaign against oral poets. . . They were effectively obliterated in England, for the most part, only with the Romantic Movement two centuries later.[25]

A useful way of construing this transitional relation is through the concept of rhetoric. Ong and Goody observe that rhetoric, as the formalization of oral speech, is one of the first instances of the codification of knowledge and skills evidenced in societies as they expand and diversify their use of writing. Rhetoric is, according to this conception, a technological development in the use of language; it reflects the increased consciousness of structural organization and the more precise ordering of words which writing makes possible.[26] It is a transitional mode of discourse:[27] while still concerned with the problems of live performance, the rhetorical process involves changing oral forms 'into something which is not simply an "oral residue" but a literary or proto-literary creation'.[28]

### Prophet as Writer: A Social Development

The appearance of oral features within written style sheds light on Ezekiel's place within Israelite prophecy. The approach taken here posits no bifurcation between a supposed oral phase of his activity and a subsequent 'scholarly' process of recording and expanding the discourse, such as Zimmerli proposes. Rather it is likely that Ezekiel composed his oracles in writing, yet in a manner deeply imbued with the forms and practices of traditional oral prophecy. This is not to say that Ezekiel's prophetic role was a private affair or a literary conceit. There are clear indications that he talked with the people

(24.18), that he was sought out as one who trafficked in the word of YHWH (20.1; 33.30-33; cf. 14.1), if not to popular satisfaction (21.5). However, the representation of Ezekiel's call to prophecy suggests that he never functioned in a purely or even primarily oral mode, as the next chapter will demonstrate. The book as a whole offers testimony to and a subtle apologetic for a fundamentally new kind of prophetic enterprise, whose locus and medium are the text.

It is necessary to try to understand the social conditions in which this new form of prophetic activity arose. Chief among them is the increasingly important place which writing was coming to play in Israelite society. As noted above, it is striking how little attention has been given to the significance of Israel's shift from primary orality toward a kind of religious and cultural activity which, certainly by the end of the exile, was deeply literate. Biblical scholars have worked so hard in this century to overcome their own writing–bound biases, crystallized into theories of documents and authors which came to dominate the field, that it may seem a step backward to reassert the peculiar contribution of writing. Yet the achievement of those who have studied writing as a cultural and hermeneutical phenomenon has been to clarify the difference between orality and writing as primary modes of creating and transmitting discourse. There is no question of going back to a naïve assumption that the bulk of Israel's traditions were produced in a mode of authorial composition resembling that prevalent in the modern world. Nor is it satisfactory, on the other hand, to see writing merely as the end of the creative process, either for individual pieces or for the tradition as a whole, with attendant implications of failure of nerve, lapse of inspiration, or both. Rather than setting oral and literary processes over against one another, with the implication that the literary historian must choose between these alternatives or at least rank them evaluatively, the task and the opportunity which modern research places before biblical scholars is to use new tools to refine our appreciation of the gradual transition between the two and the broad range of its cultural and intellectual (including theological) ramifications.[29]

From the eighth century, writing was a feature of prophecy, not only for transmission and publication at scribal hands (Isa. 8.16; Jer. 36), but also apparently as a means of illustration and emphasis within the original act of pronouncement (Isa. 8.1; Hab. 2.2; cf.

Jer. 17.1).[30] Van der Ploeg and Lemaire associate the rise of the writing prophets with what they take to be the marked increase in the use of writing in Israel and Judah during the last two centuries of the monarchy. Although van der Ploeg cautions against the view that Israelite prophets were 'authors' in the modern sense (i.e., concerned in the first instance with the production of texts), he contends that in an era of abundant writing, it is unlikely that the divine oracles would long have been entrusted solely to the oral tradition. Rather he maintains that most oracles were written down, if not by the prophets themselves, then at least during their lifetime and under their personal surveillance.[31] The extent to which this is true may well vary with different prophets. Moreover, van der Ploeg's argument is directed toward establishing the existence of a written tradition of prophecy before the exile, not toward a particular analysis of the prophetic books, and he makes no distinction among Isaiah, Jeremiah, and Ezekiel with regard to their manner of composition.

It is the purpose of this study to indicate the lines along which such a distinction can and should be made. The difference between Ezekiel and his predecessors with respect to their use of writing is not absolute: earlier prophets wrote or were closely associated with those who did.[32] Nonetheless, Ezekiel greatly exceeded his predecessors in the degree to which he exploited the potential inherent in writing. The essential difference between them consists in this: that Ezekiel's was a fundamentally literate mind, i.e., his patterns of thought and expression were shaped by habits of reading and writing. Therefore it was through him that Israelite prophecy for the first time received its *primary* impress from the new conditions and opportunities for communication created by writing.

### Literacy in Exilic Israel

Particularly important for evaluation of Ezekiel's role is what can be surmised of the relation between writing and the training and activity of priests. Unfortunately, direct evidence for formal Israelite education comes only with ben Sirach's mention of the 'house of study' (בית מדרש, 51.23). Von Rad draws upon what is known from neighboring cultures and cites 'the high level of literary achievement already apparent in the early monarchy'[33] as evidence of differentiated training for priests, scribes, court officials, Levitical preachers, and civil administrators. Lemaire argues for an elementary school system extending even to outlying fortresses such as Arad, Kadesh Barnea, and Kuntilat Ajrud, and for advanced specialized education in the capitals and large regional centers. Although Lang and Crenshaw adopt a minimalist position, maintaining the prevalence of less formal elementary education (through parental instruction or apprenticeship of children to independent teachers), both recognize the probability of specialized training at higher levels.[34] That a priest's duties demanded literacy is evident from the biblical text (Num. 5.23; Deut. 17.18; 31.24-26; Jer. 2.8), and the existence of sanctuary schools is generally acknowledged. It is likely that the Temple establishment also provided instruction in oratory and musical accompaniment.[35]

Regarding Ezekiel's own education, the little that can safely be said is sufficient to establish his credentials as a writer. A Zadokite priest,[36] he presumably prepared from an early age for the rigorous task of interpreting and pronouncing the law, and this preparation undoubtedly involved the careful study of texts. Ezekiel demonstrates 'intellectualist training'[37] which is not only exacting but broad: he draws upon historical and prophetic traditions as readily as legal ones, and the ease with which he manipulates mythic elements and calls forth vivid images bespeaks intimacy with the literary heritage of Israel and its neighbors. Although other prophets were skilled speakers, Ezekiel's Temple education promoted a structured awareness of language and led him toward an unprecedented style of prophetic discourse, one that was more consciously programmed as a communicative device.

Yet there is no need to suppose that Ezekiel's education excluded oral training, or that he would have seen his role as discontinuous with that of his predecessors. Ong's observations concerning the interaction between writing and oral learning in manuscript cultures are helpful here.[38] Until recent times, and especially before the invention of printing, memorization was an important part of the educational process even in the most literate societies. Because manuscripts are relatively cumbersome and difficult to read, they do not serve as quick reference tools; moreover, they are usually neither plentiful nor easily transportable.[39] Therefore the educated person cannot afford to be wholly dependent upon them; writing facilitates memorization and thus supports a tradition which is still internalized through largely oral means.[40] Ezekiel's text-based education gave him not only a scholar's critical command of the tradition but also a rhetor's fluency, the ability to speak with its different accents.[41]

I have already observed that advances in literacy are neither wholly private phenomena nor cultural universals, but each must be considered in the context of the society in which it occurs. It is likely, then, that the circumstances of exile also contributed to the development of this new mode of prophecy. If, as previously noted, literacy should not be seen as a direct cause of particular cognitive or social developments, it is equally true that social facts do not determine literary developments. Both forms of reductionism are misleading. The relation should be construed, not as one of causality, but rather in terms of various kinds of correspondence and reciprocal conditionality. The matter merits an historical and sociological investigation beyond the scope of this study; however, several factors may be mentioned.

First, it is evident that by the beginning of the sixth century, Israel was no longer a geographically compact community. Even before the Babylonian deportations, refugees had fled in considerable numbers to Moab, Ammon, Edom (Jer. 40.11), and especially to Egypt (Jer. 44.1),[42] and the dispersed people was never fully regathered. This movement altered the conditions for public communication, including that of the prophets. It seems that the Jerusalem Temple and the royal sanctuaries had previously been important loci for the delivery of oracles (Amos 7.13; Jer. 7.2; cf. 36.5-6), and it is likely that news of what was said at these key sites spread quickly through the land. But even before the destruction of the Temple, Jeremiah had discovered the letter as a vehicle for prophecy (Jer. 29). If the discovery did not produce an immediate change in the form of his own discourse, nonetheless it signalled an irreversible alteration in the dynamics of community life. Writing permits the extension of the community beyond the range of word-of-mouth communication. The social situation is greatly complicated by this formation of what Goody calls 'secondary group relationships',[43] and writing functions within this situation in a somewhat paradoxical way. Writing is a necessary solution to the problem of maintaining contact in a dispersed community; yet it also fosters the proliferation of such communities by enabling meaningful and even intense interaction among people who never come into personal contact. In other words, writing makes itself increasingly indispensable by simultaneously treating and perpetuating the problem of long-distance communication.

Second, exile set Ezekiel in the midst of a long-established and highly sophisticated literary culture. The Gilgamesh epic and the Code of Hammurabi attest that at least from the early second millenium, 'the perfection of writing [in Mesopotamia] had rendered possible the systematic unification of an extensive and complex material'.[44] Against those who would enshrine the oral tradition, Laessøe asserts that Mesopotamian scribes appealed to purely oral sources only as a last resort. Messengers, too, customarily read from tablets rather than relying on their own memories.[45] Hallo challenges also the stereotype of anonymous tradition reproduction within cuneiform literature, arguing for creative authorship, especially in the neo-Assyrian and neo-Babylonian periods. One of the most important questions in the history of literature is under what circumstances and by whom writing comes to be valued over living speech. Even before Ezekiel, it seems that writing was beginning to find a place within the ideology of prophecy: the written words of the prophet could wait until a time propitious for publication (Isa. 8.16); perhaps their cumulative weight would succeed where individual oracles had failed in making an impression upon the people (Jer. 36.2-3). But if Ezekiel advances writing as the primary mode of prophetic address, it is likely that he received some encouragement from the value long attached to writing in the foreign culture which now dominated his own.

The third factor which must enter into the discussion is the literate status of those whom Ezekiel addressed. Demsky and Naveh have made claims for sixth-century Israel which rival Havelock's assertions about fifth-century Athens: namely, that it was a literate society, i.e., one in which people of the lower middle class, as well as the higher and professional classes, could write.[46] Demsky cites five measures of the extent of popular literacy by the end of the Judean monarchy:

1. the high frequency of non-iconographic personal seals, in contrast to the figured seals of the eighth century;
2. the relative ubiquity of vulgar script (on jar handles and in graffiti);
3. inscriptions composed for or by craftsmen of various sorts (potters, vintners, builders, ivory joiners);

4. the flourishing of the 'writing prophets';
5. the critique of writing, showing a literate laity's awareness of the limitations of the medium (as opposed to the awe inspired among the non-literate within scribal culture) and of the dangers which arise through its abuse (e.g. Isa. 10.1-2; Jer. 8.8).

There is a general consensus, supported by inscriptional evidence, that writing was extensively used during the late monarchic period in order to meet the demands of a largely urban society with complex civil and military administrations and an elaborate cultic structure.[47] However, the case for popular literacy has not been articulated with sufficient care. While it may be true that 'few ancient Israelites were out of reach of the written word, a situation certainly facilitated by the simplicity of the alphabet',[48] this is not the same as saying that they had mastery of it. The argument for widespread literacy suffers chiefly from failure to distinguish, not only between 'passive literacy', the ability to read, and the active command of letters which writing requires,[49] but further, among various levels of active literacy. That writing in Israel was never confined solely to a scribal class seems clear (Josh. 8.32-35; 24.26), and the predominance of non-iconographic seals indicates that by the eighth century, those engaged in business and commerce of all kinds were capable at least of simple decipherment. Nonetheless, the existence of the writing prophets and the critiques of Isaiah and Jeremiah, both urbanites in close contact with royal and priestly circles, are scarcely an index of popular attitudes or the prevalence of literacy.

A useful counter to a monolithic conception of literacy is Scollon and Scollon's three-fold distinction among essayist literacy ('the ability to read and write material that is decontextualized, high in proportion of new information to old information, and internally logical', an ability chiefly gained through formal schooling),[50] pragmatic literacy (the capacity to deal with texts that are related to the immediate situation and intended for a specific, often restricted, readership; reading and writing letters or business documents are examples), and religious literacy (a 'unilateral' form of literacy which involves understanding but not writing texts as an aspect of religious, moral, or ethical instruction). The inscriptional evidence suggests that some degree of pragmatic literacy[51] was an increasingly common phenomenon during the First Temple period. On the basis of the account of Josiah's reading of the Temple scroll (2 Kgs 23), we may assume that at least by the end of the seventh century, the groundwork for 'religious literacy' was beginning to be laid in Israel: the general population was prepared to attend to a lengthy reading and accord sacred authority to a text, although there is no indication that any significant number of the people could have read it themselves.

Happily, more can be said about the Babylonian exiles than about the general Israelite population. While there is no inscriptional evidence from the Jewish community in Mesopotamia until the fifth century, a fairly high level of literacy can be inferred simply on the basis of the identity of the exiles: princes, military leaders, skilled craftsmen, royal officials, 'the notables of the land' (2 Kgs 24.14-16). Ezekiel's own presence among the exiles indicates that Temple personnel were also included. This is not to say that all Ezekiel's fellow exiles were as deeply imbued as he with literate habits—to use the Scollons' modern terminology, that they shared his degree of 'essayist literacy'. Indeed, it is likely that many of those who could read were not in the habit of doing so, except for routine and rather simple purposes. As late as the end of the Second Temple period, it seems that private reading was not necessarily practised by those who may be presumed to have been literate, as indicated by the Mishnah's proviso that, should the High Priest not be in the habit of reading Scripture, the other priests might read to him.[52] I have argued that the social implications of writing are considerable. However, in order for its impact to be felt within a culture, a uniformly high level of active literacy is less important than a general receptivity to texts and writing-based speech, a willingness to recognize these as authentic modes of discourse. Such receptivity is most likely to be found among those with some experience in reading and writing, who know how to render the particular kind of attention which texts require. It is therefore not fortuitous that Ezekiel developed a style of prophecy which the immediate audience selected for him by Nebuchadnezzar's army was especially qualified to understand, if not appreciate.

As a related matter, it is important to recall that Ezekiel's opportunities for publication differed considerably from those of modern authors. Ezekiel was not an early Tractarian, producing written texts for mass distribution and private reading. Rather he addressed a society which still had a strong network of oral channels for communication (although, as noted above, the factor of geographic separation was beginning to limit its effectiveness). Pattison observes: 'In the early history of the skill, the communal aspect of reading makes writing available to much larger audiences, since only one skilled reader is required to pass along the written information to a large group'.[53] This communal aspect may well be indicated in Ezek. 33.31: 'and they will come to you as people come', by which Greenberg understands, 'in crowds'.[54] The observations made earlier about education in a manuscript culture are relevant also to the question of publication. The values and practice of such a society are still largely informed by orality,[55] and the two modes of communication are engaged not so much in competition as in various forms of mutual support.[56]

Ong suggests that early writers often imagined themselves in an oral situation. But if texts were frequently read aloud or recited from memory (whether by their authors or by others) before an audience, then the retention of oral features is not just an ideological lag but a practical necessity. Although a written composition, even when read aloud, may make heavy demands on the audience's attention by virtue of its complexity and unfamiliarity, yet it must still be comprehensible, at least at a basic level, in a single hearing. Therefore, it is not surprising that Ezekiel makes extensive, even exaggerated use of devices associated with oral prophecy: repetition, highly visual images (e.g., the personifications of Judah and Samaria, the visions and sign acts, which are in some cases 'reifications' of images taken from earlier prophecy and psalmody), traditional formulaic language familiar to the people (e.g. the legal language of ch. 18).[57] It is a mark of his genius how far he is able to incorporate such features into a new prophetic idiom, accommodating his language to a changed discourse situation while yet producing a form of speech which can be recognized and assimilated by his audience.

## Chapter 3

## SWALLOWING THE SCROLL: THE ROLE OF THE PROPHET

Euxemus having asked Apollonius why he had written nothing yet,
though full of noble thoughts, and expressing himself so clearly and
readily, he replied: 'Because so far I have not practiced silence'.
From that time on he resolved to be mute, and did not speak at all,
though his eyes and his mind took in everything and stored it away
in his memory. Even after he had become a centenarian, he
remembered better than Simonides and used to sing a hymn in
praise of memory, in which he said that all things fade away in
time, but time itself is made fadeless and undying by recollection
(*Life of Apollonius of Tyana*, I, 14).

The cunning use of figures is peculiarly subject to suspicion. . . .
Wherefore a figure is at its best when the very fact that it is a figure
escapes attention (Longinus, *On the Sublime*, XVII, 1-2).

Ezekiel's call narrative has generally been regarded as an important
source of information about the prophet's experience and personal
character. Yet efforts to mine that information have produced a
disappointing yield. Rather than promoting a consensual view of the
prophet and his activity, the first chapters of the book have given rise
to some of the most difficult problems and, in some cases, even more
difficult solutions within Ezekiel scholarship. It must be asked
whether scholars have not been so distracted by what they have
taken to be evidence about Ezekiel as an individual that they have
often neglected the narrative's real purpose: to set forth the terms on
which we are to understand his role as prophet. That question forms
the background to the following examination of one of the book's
most explained and least illumined aspects, the phenomenon of
Ezekiel's dumbness.

## The Dumbness Motif

The need for some explanation is obvious: divine imposition of dumbness (3.26) appears to stand in direct contradiction to both the preceding charge to speak God's word to the Israelites (2.4; 3.4, 11) and the evidence of the subsequent oracles (against Judah and Jerusalem, through 24.27, and the foreign nations, 25.1–32.31) that Ezekiel fulfilled that charge. Yet the text itself acknowledges no contradiction. Despite considerable verbal activity during the period of restriction, Ezekiel reaffirms that with the arrival of the messenger announcing the fall of Jerusalem, 'my mouth was opened and I was no longer dumb' (33.22).

Attempts to resolve the difficulty can be outlined in terms of a few basic arguments. A number of early critical treatments followed the suggestion of Klostermann that the dumbness was an intermittent physical condition associated with psychological disturbance. The pathological explanation was generally superseded by Fohrer's symbolical view: Ezekiel's silence is a sign that YHWH has (temporarily) ceased to address the refractory exiles with warnings and calls to repentance. Fohrer argues further that the inference of a seven-year silence beginning immediately after the prophet's call is the result of an editorial transfer of the passage (from ch. 24?[1]) intended to give it greater prominence; the dumbness actually began only with the siege of the city. Zimmerli adopts a more extreme variant of this position, arguing that the dumbness is wholly a secondary development within the prophet's school of disciples. Lamparter and Greenberg both defend the sense of the passage in its present location by reviving the notion of intermittency. Greenberg offers a sort of hybrid of the symbolical and psychological views: the dumbness represents God's rejection of the people and reflects also the prophet's gloomy response to their hostility, an 'extreme despondency (whereby)... he lost the power for normal human contact.... Agreeably, God commands him to withdraw to his own home and be silent—except for speaking forth divine oracles, the indispensable core of his calling'.[2]

More promising are recent attempts to treat the dumbness in light of the book's larger structure, especially with respect to its representation of the prophetic office. Such a connection is encouraged by the (editorial) presence of 3.16b-21,[3] directing attention away from Ezekiel's personal condition and toward his role with respect to the people and, furthermore, reinforcing the command to speak God's word boldly and without regard for their response. On the basis of similarities of language and detail between chs. 1–2 and 3.22-27, Komlosh maintains that the prophet's call is not to be separated from these latter verses, which are related to the consecrating vision as a glimpse of the future difficulties which the prophet will encounter in fulfilling his mission. He then argues for a metaphorical and non-coercive interpretation of the restriction as it relates to the frequently attested popular rejection of the prophetic word of reproof (cf. e.g. Isa. 29.21; Amos 5.10; Mic. 2.6). The notice in 3.26 is not a command but a warning of the opposition and deafness which Ezekiel should expect to encounter in fulfilling his charge to prophesy. Such a reading, however, actually weakens the good case for a primary connection between the call and the dumbness by making the latter depend, not upon the initiative of YHWH—although the book represents that initiative as standing behind the call as well as every subsequent act and speech of the prophet—but upon the anticipated reaction of the people: Ezekiel is not to be mediator (איש מוכיח, 3.26) for the house of Israel, because they will not receive him as such.

The divine initiative is upheld in Wilson's proposal that the dumbness functions within the call narrative as a figure for divine curtailment of the prophetic role: unlike his predecessors, Ezekiel is not to mediate an exchange between Israel and its God.

> The implication of 3.26 is that in the dialogue which Yahweh carries on with his people through the prophet, communication can now move in only one direction: from Yahweh to the people. . . . The people in turn may either hear or refuse to hear, but they may not turn the divine oracle into a dialogue.[4]

Yet Wilson finds a connection between the prophet's call and his dumbness only at the editorial level. The motive for insertion of 3.22-27 and the consequent narrowing of the prophet's function is apologetic: if Ezekiel had intervened for Israel, the disaster of destruction and exile would not have happened; therefore, he must have been legitimately prevented from performing his expected task of mediation.

These various treatments all fail to some degree to account for the biblical text, in which there is no qualification of the dumbness as (following Klostermann, Lamparter, Greenberg) intermittent or (following Komlosh, Greenberg) dependent upon the people's prior rejection of the prophet. Moreover, those who read the dumbness wholly as an editorial device do so at the expense of the text's synchronic intelligibility (so Fohrer, Zimmerli) or at least do not recognize Ezekiel's dumbness as a fundamental element in the representation of his prophetic function. That it is such an element can be demonstrated (along the lines indicated by Wilson) and, furthermore, anchored, not merely in an apologetic intention of the editors, but in the whole structure of the book as it attests to a significant development in the conception of the prophetic role and in the status of the divine word itself. Specifically, I maintain that Ezekiel's dumbness is a metaphor for the move toward textualization of Israel's sacred traditions; the figure stands over all that follows to designate this prophet's career as a critical juncture in the history of revelation.

The imposition of dumbness is not, of course, the only peculiarity of Ezekiel's call. The first act of obedience demanded of the prophet is consumption of a meal which is repellent both in form and content: he must eat the written word of judgment against Israel (2.8–3.3). Ezekiel's immediate predecessor also had occasion to 'swallow' the word of God as part of his equipment for service. Jeremiah's use of the metaphor (15.16; cf. 1.9; Deut. 18.18) suggests already the autonomy of the revealed word with respect to the prophet. It is a thing encountered (נמצאו), which the prophet takes into himself, only to learn how quickly that word escapes his control (17.15) and proves to be a source, no longer of delight, but of anguish (20.8-9) and bitter dispute (28.1-11). Moreover, the ingested word eventually passes out of Jeremiah in a form hitherto unknown for prophecy. It becomes a scroll, a collection of oracles not only resistant to destruction (36.27-32) but also capable of maintaining its existence and asserting its authority independent of the speaker (36.5-8).

The book of Jeremiah is important evidence that prophetic speech was coming to be associated, not just with a vivid moment of revelation, but also with a tradition of fixed words. At the same time, through the process of inscription, the revealed word was being gradually detached from the circumstances of its original utterance and freed from dependence on personal contact between the prophet and his audience. Nonetheless, the figure of the word which is met, ingested, and ultimately textualized is here overshadowed by other figures—notably, those of fire and hammer (5.14; 20.9; 23.29)—more consistent with Jeremiah's highly personalized account of his struggle with the immediate, irresistible power of the divine word.

The metaphor of ingestion has progressed greatly by the time of its reappearance as the prominent figure in Ezekiel's call narrative, coloring any conception of his life as prophet. This time verbal consumption is not a casual, voluntary gesture; it is the precondition for public service. These words are not merely encountered; their authenticity and authority are unmistakable, for they come directly from the hand of God. But most strikingly, there is no longer any ambiguity about the form in which the prophet receives the edible revelation. It comes to Ezekiel already *as a text*. This is the form in which he must claim his inheritance and the basis on which he must make his own contribution to the tradition of faithful witness.

The figure of the scroll points to an important difference between the two prophets with respect to the primacy of writing. Jeremiah resorts to writing on two occasions, and in both cases the motivation for adopting this strategy is clear and seems to mark an exception to his ordinary practice of oral delivery. First, he sends a letter to his fellow Israelites now carried into exile, far beyond the reach of his voice. Second, he produces a scroll for Baruch to read to the Jerusalemites in his stead, since Jeremiah has been barred from the Temple compound and therefore effectively denied a public hearing. Moreover, there seems to be some hope that the cumulative testimony of all God's words spoken through Jeremiah will at last make some impact on the Judeans.[5] Writing the oracles is here a supplement to oral prophecy and, in the last analysis, a counsel of despair. For Ezekiel, however, the scroll functions quite differently: it gives the first impetus to prophecy. It is not surprising that, with a mind shaped and honed by the study of sacred texts, and living under conditions which greatly increased the importance of writing for public communication, this man should from the beginning have conceived his commission to prophesy in a manner congruent with the concept of God's word as text.

Wilson has pointed to the narrowing of the prophetic role as evidence in the watchman image and the restrictions on Ezekiel's movement and speech. But the narrowness of Ezekiel's function relative to his predecessors is actually apparent from the first moment of God's address, when he is appointed specifically and solely for messenger speech (2.4; cf. 3.11). Immediately after he swallows the scroll, the command seems to be reinforced. Greenberg interprets the unusual phrase -ב דבר (3.4) thus: '"speak in a particular form.". . . Here the nuance (absent in the commonplace *dibber 'et* of 2.7) seems to be verbatim repetition of the message—an aspect of absolute obedience'.[6] But the inference of the odd usage can be drawn more precisely: it is not that Ezekiel is called to more stringent obedience in speaking God's word than were earlier prophets, but that what is required for obedience has changed. Jeremiah's call to prophetic service is demanding precisely in its breadth: 'to pluck up and to pull down, to obliterate and to destroy, to build and to plant' (1.10). Further specification of his call comes in the form of images of confrontation. Jeremiah is called out onto the contested ground between God and Israel, to wage his campaign of destruction and restoration with words (1.17). That role leads Jeremiah to exploit the full range of traditional speech forms, both prophetic and psalmic, in castigating the people, calling them to repent, and lamenting his own fate as the anguished bearer of the devastating word. This would appear to be the very opposite of the compulsion laid upon Ezekiel. His call leads, not to urgent appeal, but to confinement and dumbness. Ezekiel must fall 'silent' and let the scroll which he has swallowed speak through him.

Several aspects of the figure are suggestive of the milieu in which Ezekiel was called to prophesy. The first is the notion of ingestion as a means of appropriating the divine word. In an anthropological study contrasting the passive pedagogical systems of modern society with the 'rhythmo-catechetical' system of the Palestinian rabbis, Jousse emphasizes the importance of memorable gestures and figures:

> In a rhythmo-catechetical environment. . ., we again find, always and everywhere, this concern for replaying, for repeating an echo, for 'mishnaizing' all the corporal, manual, and oral gestures of the one who gives instruction. . . . In effect, in an environment of oral style, one takes the words of the instructor into one's mouth and eats them.[7]

He cites the scroll incident in Ezekiel as an instance of *manducation mémorisation* and notes that the figure is comprehensible only to those sensitive to the palpable 'texture' of oral language (cf. Pss. 34.9; 40.9; Prov. 9.4). Jousse's remarks are not a denial of the importance of writing (which could hardly be maintained for the rabbinic period) but rather a reminder that in cultures still committed to the importance of orality, especially in the educational process, memorization, far from being displaced by the use of writing, is actually aided by it.[8] Indeed, he observes that words used as gestures ('Let there be light!', 'This is my body; take, eat!') do not lose their sense of primary efficacy even in writing—an idea which is of great significance for understanding Ezekiel's sign-actions.

It is noteworthy also that the scroll incident is framed on both sides by injunctions which seem to suggest extreme precision in delivery of the divine word (2.4; 3.4[9]). This can in part be connected with the highly charged religio-political situation, which made prophecy in the twilight of the monarchy a business even more risky than usual (cf. Jer. 20.1-6; 28.15-17; 36.26; 37.11-15; 43.1-7), and with what might be called Ezekiel's passion for validation.[10] But it may also point to a change in the prophetic process itself, i.e., employment of a medium which facilitated precise transmission of YHWH's word, not only by the prophet, but also by subsequent generations. There is some evidence that verbatim reproduction of lengthy discourse seems to be highly valued and, to a great extent, possible only in literate societies, whereas oral cultures tend to favor thematic recitation.[11]

Third, the figure of the dumbness is supported and interpreted by the accompanying figure, that of confinement. It is useful to recall Ewald's notion of Ezekiel's 'solitary prophetic meditation',[12] for it is directly connected with his view that this prophet is in the first instance a writer. In his banishment from public activity, 'the prophetic activity of Hézeqiél's own mind' becomes all the more intense.

> As he now reflects on that, it seems to him as he writes as though
> that also was the result of a higher arrangement, for the purpose of
> a preliminary schooling and strengthening by the private exercise
> of his prophetic foreboding, prediction, and literary faculty.[13]

Ewald correctly recognizes Ezekiel's confinement as being the precondition for his development as a writer. Yet one may go further and say that the confinement represents not only an externally imposed limitation, but also the condition which the task of writing itself demands. While social withdrawal affords the opportunity for reflection and thus facilitates writing, it is equally true that the need or desire to write provides the impetus for withdrawal. But there is no necessity, finally, to choose between the two interpretations. Writing seems to have been the fundamental mode of Ezekiel's prophecy, one to which he was suited by both training and disposition. If another means of proclamation was attempted and failed, we are given no indication of that, either in the narrative or the speeches, whose form is in many cases inexplicable except as employing the techniques of writing in their original formation.[14] However, as I have argued, the adoption of this mode was influenced also by certain constraints and opportunities in Ezekiel's social circumstances. The very indefiniteness of the expression in 3.25[15] suggests an ambiguity regarding the agent of his confinement. Because of the suffix on בתוכם ('in the midst of them'), Greenberg excludes the possibility of reading the verb נתנו as an indefinite active form with passive meaning,[16] yet he does allow for a figurative reading of the verse: 'the public repulsion toward you is so great, it has as good as driven you off the streets and confined you to your quarters'.[17] However, in conjunction with the absence of a personal subject here, recurrence of the expression a few verses later with God as the subject (נתתי עליך עבותים; 'I have placed cords upon you', 4.8) would seem to reflect back on this usage and suggest a fundamental divine intention behind both. In accordance with the overwhelmingly theocentric focus of the book, Ezekiel's confinement and dumbness are to be understood as proceeding from God's initiative, although in a manner responsive to the situation in which he must function.

In equating Ezekiel's dumbness with the ban on serving as mediator (איש מוכיח), Wilson's study advances the notion that the people, too, are constrained by the new limits imposed upon the prophet. The shocking oath, חי-אני אם-אדרש לכם ('By my life,[18] I will not respond to your inquiry', 20.3; cf. 20.31; 14.3), avers that they no longer have a legitimate channel, in the person of Ezekiel, for seeking special revelations or making their appeal to God. The shift from an interactive communications situation to a unidirectional flow represents a major reinterpretation of the prophetic role.[19] The significance of its occurrence in the career of this prophet may be illumined by considering the degree to which interaction is a feature of various kinds of discourse situations, both written and oral.

The most obvious form of interactive discourse is, of course, conversation between individuals. The fact that it is a 'turn-taking' mode of communication enables negotiation, clarification, and mutual adjustment of positions. It might be said that the most important aspect of such situations is not the subject matter but the personal interaction itself, or that meaning only emerges through the interactive process. However, as the roles of addresser and addressee become more fully distinguished, there is generally less allowance for negotiation. While it is not necessarily true that the problem of meaning receives correspondingly greater attention, the way in which sense is made does change. The addresser is obliged and privileged to make sense in a largely unilateral fashion. Such formalized discourse situations are found in oral contexts (e.g. academic lectures, political speeches, sermons) as well as with written media (e.g. schooltexts and various other kinds of expository prose). Contrariwise, writing may seem to resemble live speech in permitting a kind of negotiation. Some texts, especially those of the category usually designated as 'literature' (in the narrow sense of artistic creations), allow for a range of applications and interpretive possibilities. But where it is appropriate to speak of permission or allowance, the possibility of restriction is also implied. What is written is fixed, at least in one version, and the author is rarely present with the text to explain or emend. Moreover, the voice of the text is strengthened by the fact that the writer has generally devoted to the task of expression time and pains which few speakers allow. Literary creations must be recognized for what they are, calculated exercises of power, and that they are effective as such is evidenced in the popular view: 'It must be true; I read it in a book'. The author's unavailability, as well as the fact that an adequate answer can only be rendered obliquely—i.e., through production of another text—places the reader or hearer in a position of (in Ricoeur's terms) fundamental inequality *vis-à-vis* the text.

The figure of confinement and dumbness expresses a drastic curtailment of the prophet's role, one which restricts prophet and people alike. Obedience for Ezekiel does not mean, as it did for Jeremiah, speaking as the living mouth of God, testing his own fresh utterances for their worth (Jer. 15.19—significantly, immediately after his eating of the divine words). At this juncture in Israel's history, there is no need—no room—for a new prophetic message. The words for this situation have already been proclaimed (by Jeremiah?[20]) and inscribed: words of lamentation and moaning and woe (2.10). God's judgment on Jerusalem is a matter of record. From now until the fall of the city, there are no genuinely new oracles; this is the time for performance of the word which has been decreed (12.28; cf. Jer. 1.12). The fixity of the scroll of judgment admits of no negotiation or alteration in response to the people's appeal. Ezekiel must fall dumb and let the scroll that he swallowed speak through him. But no more than with Jeremiah does the act of ingestion give him control over the divine word. On the contrary, during the period of dumbness, Ezekiel is merely the vehicle of the divinely authored text.

With Ezekiel, the goal of prophecy undergoes a profound shift. No longer is it aimed at opening the ears of the people and averting disaster (cf. Jer. 25.3; 26.2-3; 36.2-3). That possibility is foreclosed, and now the function of the prophet is simply to make known to Israel the author of judgment and the just grounds for its execution (16.2; 20.4). The divine recognition formula (וירעתם/וירעו כי אני יי, 'and you/they shall know that I am YHWH'), which recurs continually throughout the book, and the related formula, וירעו כי נביא היה בתוכם ('and they shall know that a prophet was in their midst'; 2.5; 33.33), show how completely the role of the prophet and the course of history are determined by that primary intention of God.

The test of any interpretation must finally be whether it illumines works in their entirety. It has been argued here that the connection between Ezekiel's call—particularly the swallowing of the scroll—and his dumbness is a primary relation to be understood in terms of the emergence of Scripture in Israel and the effect of that development on the prophet's historical ministry. If that is indeed the case, then the interpretation must be found compatible with the whole structure of the text. Particularly significant in this regard is the book's inference that Ezekiel's dumbness was total (in whatever sense it applied) but temporary. Therefore it must be possible to show that there is some absolute difference between the ways the prophet functioned before and after the lifting of the restriction.

A clue to the essential role which the figure of dumbness plays in the representation of Ezekiel's prophetic career is the fact that later references to it occur at key junctures in the text. An anticipation of its termination concludes the long series of denunciations and threats against Judah and Jerusalem (24.27), and the ban is finally lifted when news of the city's fall reaches Babylon (33.22).[21] Now at last, when the word of destruction has been performed, there is a chance for a new word to be spoken—perhaps, moreover, to be heard. And indeed, there is a change of tone at this point in the text. The whole force of the first twenty-four chapters is to convict Israel of the extent of its sin and the righteousness of God's judgment. Although there is no possibility that the judgment will be reversed, nonetheless it is necessary that Israel be brought to recognition of its own deserving (especially through the lurid portraits of chs. 16 and 23). Only this recognition, more humiliating than the destruction itself, can serve as the basis of a renewed relationship with YHWH (6.8-10; 16.62-63; 20.43-44). Seen in close conjunction with the dramatic oracles and visions of restoration which follow (chs. 36–48), ch. 33 marks a change in the discourse situation. Here, as so often in this book, the prophet identifies his target by a citation of popular speech: 'Our transgressions and our sins are upon us and in them we are rotting away; how then shall we live?' (33.10). This outcry is the first indication that Israel has begun to perceive the extent of its own wretchedness, and YHWH charges the prophet to respond with a rare appeal for repentance (33.11; cf. 18.30-31). Ezekiel is still engaged more in diatribe than in consolation; the oracles in ch. 33 are directed wholly toward demolishing the corrupt tenets of popular theology (33.17, 24-29) and showing clearly wherein lie the seat of responsibility and the possibility of restoration (33.12-16). Although the message is not new (cf. ch. 18), it would seem that the precondition for its acceptance is only now met: through fulfillment of the word of doom, the people learn 'that there has been a prophet in their midst' (33.33). On the other side of disaster, God opens the prophet's mouth[22] and fills it with new words.

It must be stressed that the change in the prophet's way of speaking is not primarily a response to the people's greater receptivity. The opening of his mouth, like the dumbness, proceeds entirely from God's initiative. Indeed, the fact that the text specifically designates the opening as having occurred before the arrival of the refugee (33.21-22) underscores the divine initiative; this is not Ezekiel's reaction to the news of the fall. The crucial point here is that Ezekiel speaks differently—prophesies, in a sense, for the first time—because this is genuinely new revelation. He is no longer constrained by the scroll which he swallowed, because the limits of that text have been exceeded. The word of judgment has been

fulfilled, the 'laments and moaning and woe' have all been uttered,
and now a new word is needed. The regnant theological system
asserting the eternality of David's covenant has been razed along
with his city. Standing in that void, Ezekiel has a creative ministry to
perform. He must speak the first word of hope to the exiles after the
destruction; he is to articulate the vision on which the future can be
built.

### Archival Speech

In view of what has been said about Ezekiel's reponsibility to
establish the grounds of the disaster rather than to fend it off, it is not
surprising that he should evidence a concern for validation of this
unusual (and, from the people's perspective, doubtless disappointing)
prophetic function. That concern finds expression in the formula
וידעו כי נביא היה בתוכם ('and they shall know that a prophet was in
their midst'), which occurs in the call narrative (2.5) and again at the
time when word of the city's fall reaches Babylon (33.33), thus
marking the boundaries of the first phase of Ezekiel's prophecy. In
the first occurrence of the phrase, the divine speech shows what
appears to be a sovereign disregard (אם־ישמעו ואם־יחדלו 'whether they
hear or not', 2.5) for whether the prophet's immediate audience will
attend seriously to the warning he speaks; in the second instance, it is
evident that they have not. The crucial thing is this: that the warning
be documented, that the record of God's timely speaking be
established. The same notion underlies the reiterated watchman
image (3.16b-21; 33.1-9), which also frames the speeches belonging
to the period before the fall. Far from revealing the 'irrationality' of
YHWH's desire to hold back the doom which is divinely decreed,[23]
the image demonstrates the methodical justice of this God who
warns before striking, though knowing that the warning will be more
effective in retrospect—to answer the question of theodicy—than in
prospect.

   Complementary to the documentation of God's speech is Ezekiel's
concern that he himself should be recognized as one who does not
speak on his initiative, but rather is sent (3.5). It is as expressions of
this concern that one must understand the prophet's infrequent
allusions to his own response to revelation, his reactions of awe
(1.28), desolation (3.15), horror (9.8; 11.13[24]). These comments are
less useful as clues to the prophet's psychological condition than as

self-conscious attestations to his status as the unwilling bearer of the message rather than its author. Constant repetition of the messenger formula, כה אמר יי ('thus says YHWH'), keeps Ezekiel's audience mindful of his subordinate status. With a passion for veracity which shows him to be both prophet and scholar, Ezekiel even 'footnotes' his own learning process within the revelatory experience (10.13, 20).

A particularly interesting feature of Ezekiel's propensity for documentation is the recurrent date formulae which (excepting 40.1) appear among the doom speeches. A number of earlier scholars (Hitzig, Hölscher, Torrey, more recently Irwin) regarded the dates as dubious or clearly spurious. However, investigation was reopened with publication of Weidner's report on cuneiform ration records mentioning Jehoiakin (variously spelled), king of Judah, and his five sons. Albright argues thus for the authenticity of Ezekiel's dating system: not only the exiles but also the Babylonians regarded Jehoiakin as the legitimate king of Judah, 'held in reserve for possible restoration if circumstances should seem to require it'.[25] Because it was unsafe for the exiles to flaunt their loyalty by dating from Jehoiakin's regnal years, they dated from his captivity; for a post-exilic editor to have invented such a system would have been absurd. Freedy and Redford adduce evidence from biblical, Babylonian, and Egyptian sources to consolidate the argument that the dates (with the exception of 24.1, borrowed from 2 Kgs 25.1) are an original feature of the book.

Zimmerli draws a connection between Ezekiel's dates and the use of writing in Babylonian legal transactions, where a contract's validity was based on several factors: the fact of its being written, naming of witnesses, appending of an oath, and exact reference to a date. Certainly he is correct in perceiving that the dates are an authenticating device, and the connection with the inscriptional process is valuable.[26] It would seem that Ezekiel was moving prophecy in the direction of archival speech, marking and filing the evidence, documenting the case that the divine word was indeed delivered in due time, though the warning was not heeded.[27] In this light, Zimmerli's further observation that 'in the dating there is expressed unmistakably the conviction that the word of Yahweh. . . represented a message of God for a particular occasion'[28] calls for some qualification. The question to be asked is whether receipt of the revelation, composition or deliver *on* a specified date constitutes an intention to speak *to* a particular situation.

Several plausible attempts have been made to connect Ezekiel's dates with events known from other sources.[29] These may well illumine the historical background, but they are less useful in determining the function of the speeches. For it is remarkable that, despite their careful documentation, the dated addresses are nowhere represented as spoken in direct response to an historical event or a question concerning one. Rather, when the elders follow the normal procedure of coming to the prophet to inquire of YHWH,[30] they are vehemently rebuffed (14.3; 20.3, 31). The crucial point to be observed is that Ezekiel never returns a direct answer to a question of immediate political relevance. This prophet effectively announces the end of oracular inquiry in Israel. He cuts the Gordian knot of true and false prophecy by declaring that any prophet so beguiled (יפתה, 14.9) as to conduct business as usual, or any patron who thinks to resort at will to the former channel of revelation (14.7-8; cf. Jer. 29.15), will be expelled from the house of Israel. From now on, the divine word will be given solely at God's initiative.[31]

There is a further sense in which prophecy has ceased to be an immediately responsive form of communication. Here it is highly significant that the speech forms throughout the book are generally very far removed from those of oracular pronouncement. Freedy and Redford comment perceptively on the effect of the historical survey in ch. 20:

> [Ezekiel] refashions the traditional Heilsgeschichte to make a point
> in contemporary Weltgeschichte. The recital itself thus becomes
> metaphorical rather than literal, and so do the contents of the
> judgment oracle (vv. 30-31) which concludes the piece.[32]

It is reasonable to suppose that the elders came to Ezekiel (20.1) seeking quite particular information regarding current affairs,[33] but they are flatly denied satisfaction on those terms. Ezekiel obliges them, not with a practical answer, but with an historical narrative, and that of an extremely imaginative kind.[34] A later chapter will deal in detail with the function of this kind of discourse, but a few remarks are necessary here.

Narrative is an oblique form of speech in two respects. First, it neither aims at the momentary concerns of an addressee nor emanates directly from a prior assertion or question. Narratives are prime examples of what Pratt calls 'display texts', characterized particularly by detachability from an immediate speech context and also by 'tellability', an inner coherence which enables them to be used appropriately and comprehensibly in a variety of circumstances. Often they are simply volunteered, bring a new agenda into the situation of telling, demanding attention on their own grounds and merit. A second and related aspect of the narrative's oblique character is that it is designed, not primarily to convey information, but to provoke thought and offer insight into unusual or problematic situations. Therefore it is inherently frustrating to anyone seeking an oracle, i.e. a yes-or-no answer or a pithy prediction. Narratives serve an explanatory function, guiding the audience to a certain conclusion, but their means are indirect and comprehensible only to those who are themselves willing to make an imaginative effort.

The fact that Ezekiel is the first to elaborate narrative forms in the service of prophecy confirms the impression gained through study of the dumbness motif: that his book witnesses to a kind of prophetic discourse never before heard in Israel. Furthermore, it evidences a kind of detachment from a particular set of historical circumstances which has been shown to be especially characteristic of writing. In this connection, the sublime disregard for whether or not the word is heeded at the time of proclamation—expressed, significantly, on either side of the scroll-swallowing incident (2.7; 3.12)—becomes comprehensible. The prophets' urgency to break through Israel's deafness, which reached a crescendo in Jeremiah, is gone. The point of orientation for the prophetic word has shifted from crisis to archive. Preserved as text, God's word is no longer frustrated by the intransigence of any generation; it can wait until such time as it may be heard.

There is another way in which Ezekiel might be said to develop prophetic speech in archival forms, evidenced in his extensive dependence on earlier tradition. The form-critical and traditio-historical work of Zimmerli has impressively demonstrated the close and detailed connections, including both motifs and speech forms, between Ezekiel and the Holiness Code. Even more striking is Ezekiel's reliance on but also eclecticism with respect to the prophetic tradition. Like Isaiah but in more elaborate form, he combines his narrative of a personal call (cf. Jer. 1) with a vision of the heavenly council (cf. 1 Kgs 22). More than any other writing prophet, Ezekiel revitalizes the concepts of pre-classical prophecy: the hand of God falling upon the prophet at the onset of a trance with exceptional physical or sensory results (1.3; 3.22; 8.1; 33.22; 37.1; 40.1; cf. 1 Kgs 18.46; 2 Kgs 3.15), the phenomenon of far-sightedness (chs. 8–11; cf. 2 Kgs 26), רוח or (more rarely) רוח אלהים operating almost as an independent force upon the prophet (3.12, 14; 8.3; 11.1, 24; 43.5; cf. 2 Kgs 2.16). Ezekiel's language and imagery shimmer with reflections from the poetic and prophetic sources, and are at times intelligible only against that background. Most numerous are the points of contact with Jeremianic tradition. Moreover, it is noteworthy that the images which Ezekiel picks up from his older contemporary in several instances represent aspects of the prophetic office: not only ingestion of the divine word but also the unheeded watchman (Jer. 6.17; Ezek. 3.17-21; 33.1-9), the fortified prophet (Jer. 1.18 and 15.20; used as a metaphor, Ezek. 3.8-9, as a sign-act, ch. 4). A related phenomenon is Ezekiel's transformation of metaphorical figures from other texts into sign-actions or fully articulated visions: Isaiah's 'razor hired across the river' (7.20) is realized in Ezekiel's shaving (5.1); the parched, scattered bones of the psalms (Pss. 53.6; 102.4; 141.7) come alive in the vision on the plain (ch. 37).

Other prophets engage in direct and often heated exchange with various of their contemporaries—kings and priests, disciples and rival prophets—but Ezekiel appears primarily in conversation with the tradition. Like a creative archivist, he desires not only to preserve the treasures of the past but also to make them available and meaningful in the present. Even his disputation speeches are aimed as much at the tradition as at the people, purging it of its useless elements (12.22-28; 18.2-4) and correcting disastrous misinterpretations (33.24-29). The narratives in chs. 16, 23, and especially 20 show also how far Ezekiel is willing to go in producing a highly schematized and almost unrecognizably revisionist history.

That Ezekiel has carefully crafted his own contribution to the tradition is indisputable, attested not only in the construction of individual pieces but, even more importantly, in the way words, phrases, themes, and images are replayed to create a series of echoes throughout the book. Something of the process by which Ezekiel constructed his text is illumined through application of Seidel's principle concerning a chiastic method of intra-Scriptural reference:

'The prophet who makes use of the phrases of the verse hovering before his eyes, uses them in reverse order, bringing forward the later phrase in that verse and putting the earlier one later.'[35] The phrase 'hovering before his eyes' (המרחף לנגד עיניו) indicates that this is an instance of a writer working from previously composed material. Although Seidel's work is confined to Isaiah's use of the psalms, Weiss discovers the same principle in other prophetic passages, including Ezek. 8.12 and 9.9; 11.3 and 11.7, 11; 16.3 and 45; 16.6-7 and 22; 21.8 and 9; 21.9 and 10; 23.6 and 12; and especially 34.4 and 16. Greenberg (following Abarbanel) shows how the vision description in chs. 8 and 10 reverses the order of narration in ch. 1 and notes also several instances of inversion—both within the chapter itself and with respect to Deut. 24.16—in ch. 18.

Ezekiel's self-consciousness as a tradent is evidenced also in the genre-designations he attaches to the speech forms he employs (16.44; 17.2; 19.1; 27.2, 32; 32.2a, *et al.*), and especially where he marks them for use and re-use (19.14b; 32.16). But the most striking literary fact is that, apparently within the period of his own prophetic activity, Ezekiel saw his words becoming fixed within the tradition. The crucial passage in this regard is 29.17-21, dated to the twenty-seventh year of the exile, promising Egypt to Nebuchadnezzar as compensatory booty for his disappointment over Tyre. That the passage is present at all has important implications for our understanding of Ezekiel's prophetic role. For it stands as an update to his original prophecies against Tyre (chs. 26–28, dated to the eleventh year, 26.1) and indicates that anticipation of the enemy's reaping of Tyre's vast wealth (26.12) was not subject to direct emendation in the light of subsequent history (namely, the exhaustion of its wealth through Nebuchadnezzar's thirteen-year siege, 586/85-573/72[36]). Within only sixteen years, Ezekiel's words had ceased to be malleable, even by himself; they had entered into the prophetic canon. The speed with which this fixity was achieved doubtless reflects Ezekiel's move in instituting the text as a primary vehicle of prophecy; for, as has been shown, once promulgated, a text escapes the control of its author and becomes public property. This remarkable passage serves as a caution against a privatized view of Ezekiel's writing activity, but more than that, it represents a serious challenge to easy assumptions about the degree to which the text was subject to manipulation by the prophet's followers and imitators.

Even Ezekiel was constrained by the text he produced; leaving the testimony of his own mistaken prediction was the price the writer-prophet paid for what his speech gained thereby in authority.

## The Prophetic Role: Alternate Models

This proposal that Ezekiel was distinguished from previous prophets by his performance of a function which was in large part archival—documenting present events, consciously systematizing and supplementing the tradition—stands in contrast to two other current conceptions. The first of these, recently put forth in several studies by Bernhard Lang, is important as a serious reconsideration of the nature of Ezekiel's prophetic role. Lang opposes what he takes to be the standard view of Ezekiel as a 'fatalistic doomseer and a mere pedagogue' with the picture of 'a prophetic politician'[37] embroiled in the heated controversy between the peace and rebellion parties in Babylon. The consistent aim of both oracles and sign-actions is to present a forceful argument, directed first to the exiled leaders of the pro-Egyptian faction and through them to Zedekiah, against rebellion in Jerusalem. Although Lang's work is often insightful, his characterization of Ezekiel's prophetic role can be criticized on several points.

First, the idea, taken from Max Weber, of the prophetic collections as 'the earliest directly topical pamphlet literature known to us'[38] is very unsatisfactory. It imports into the ancient world a modern concept without taking account of the fact that pamphleteering as a cheap and ready means of reaching the masses was quite unthinkable before the invention of the printing press. But even if it be supposed that the material was read aloud, it is more than doubtful whether the degree of literary complexity evidenced by Ezekiel's writings is suitable for the purposes of public agitation. The next chapter's examination of how Ezekiel's prophecy identifies and involves an audience will provide fuller grounds for this assertion.

Second, as has been argued above, there are strong indications that Ezekiel differed from other prophets precisely in not holding out the possibility that disaster might be averted. The indictment of the bloody city in ch. 22, a second-person address which complements the third-person narrative in ch. 20 by setting forth the grounds for the destruction, illustrates the contrast. Ezekiel picks up from older prophecy the image of Israel as corrupted silver (Isa. 1.22, 25). But, whereas in Isaiah the image is couched in the context of a divine appeal and promise of transformation (i.e., successful refining), Ezekiel emphasizes that God's smelting action will only confirm the essential worthlessness of the base material (cf. ch. 15).[39] The lists of offenses by Israel's kings, priests, and prophets (vv. 6-12, 25-29) are comprehensive retrospectives which admit of neither defense nor remedy.[40]

Third, Lang's implication (based on his reading of 33.1-9 as describing the office of an urban military commisioner) that Ezekiel's role as watchman depends upon ongoing social approval is not supported by the text. The role of the humanly appointed watchman (v. 2) is presented as an analogy, but it is also clearly distinguished from Ezekiel's own appointment by God (נתתיך צופה, 'I have appointed you a watchman', v. 7; cf. 3.17). The contrast is deepened by the change in description of the threat from the military sphere (the sword and the horn, vv. 2-6) to the moral/theological one of the priest (vv. 7-9). The inference is that Ezekiel's commission to prophesy proceeds solely from God, and there is no indication that his function is in any way influenced by the people's response.

It is curious that, although Lang considers the Babylonian exile to be the watershed between the prophetic period and the rise of scribes or scholars as the dominant figures in Israelite religion, he makes no attempt to connect the exilic prophets with this transition.[41] Yet all the characteristics by which he identifies the intellectual/scholar (mastery of a complex body of knowledge and cognitive skills; a long period of study and training; engagement in areas such as teaching, preaching, and the arts; and exercise of informal or charismatic authority) are surely true of Ezekiel. It is easy to see this prophet drawing close to the line which Lang sets between prophet and scribe (a line which probably remained wavy well into the post-exilic period):

> However tradition-bound a prophet's oracle may be, it is a new revelation. For the scribe, the living spirit has crystallized into a book which permits of no new revelation. Although the charisma is embodied in a book and thereby 'tamed', it still retains its supernatural quality. One is not surprised, then, to hear that some of the scriptural scholars act like prophets. On the other hand, the difference is characteristic: the oracle religion becomes a book

religion, the direct experience of revelation becomes the knowledge thereof, and the place of the charismatic prophet is taken by the charismatic teacher.[42]

It would seem that Lang has prepared much of the ground for appreciation of Ezekiel's importance in the transition from prophet to scribe as socially developed forms. Yet his failure to acknowledge this constitutes an important inconsistency in his position. For he admits that Ezekiel, despite his political concerns, finally remains a utopian, never addressing strategic questions or showing the way into the future. It is likely that, while Ezekiel's self-representation and others' view of him are still informed by the old ideology of the prophet, active on the streets, at the holy places, and in royal circles, he is actually moving prophecy toward the intellectual mode which Lang recognizes for the Hellenistic scribes: passionately concerned that their ideas be put into practice, yet exercising their charisma largely in the teaching circle and at the desk.

If my view of the prophet departs on one side from the claim that he is a political activist, it is on the other removed from various kinds of privatistic interpretations. These by definition rarely involve consideration of the prophetic role as such but rather present a personality profile of Ezekiel as 'a great individualist and a hero of the spirit',[43] an ecstatic, or, less flatteringly, as hypersensitive, neurotic, hysterical. Clinically oriented psychological characterizations usually find their proof texts in the reports of the visions and the sign-actions. This tradition of interpretation reached its acme in a 'case study' by Broome, who diagnosed the prophet as a paranoid schizophrenic showing symptoms of catatonia, alalia, delusions of persecution and grandeur, narcissistic masochism, sexual regression and gender confusion, psychotic withdrawal. While Broome's confidence in the exegetical power of medical science is exceptional, even so responsible a scholar as Gunkel resorts to explanations such as nervous derangement or an irrepressible unconscious for antics and images whose purpose or meaning is unclear (e.g. binding, dumbness).[44]

Greenberg's refined approach also includes frequent surmises about Ezekiel's psychological condition. For example, citing Freedman to the effect that 'Ezekiel's account is more a spiritual diary of personal experiences of God and his inner reaction to it than a record of objective occurrences',[45] he continues: 'In accordance with his

tendency to extremes, he carries Jeremiah's gloomy unsociability...
to its last degree. ....'[46] Objections must be raised to this view. First,
Freedman's remark is open to criticisms similar to those levelled at
the once popular estimation of Jeremiah's confessions as a purely
personal record unconnected with the prophet's public activity.[47]
The fact that Ezekiel's whole book is composed from a first-person
perspective sharpens the issue. For if that makes it a spiritual diary,
then it is doubtful whether Ezekiel can legitimately be called a
prophet at all. While it is true that Ezekiel 'for the most part lives in a
separate world',[48] I suggest that this testifies less to his character
than to the circumstances in which he was contrained to work as a
prophet and the literary means he devised to perform that function.
The book he produced may accordingly be seen, not indeed as 'a
record of objective occurrences' (begging the question of whether there
can ever be such a thing), but as an imaginatively constructed
literary work which also, and not incidentally, serves as an *apologia*
for that irreversible shift in the prophetic role.

### Sign-Actions

The sign-actions deserve special attention from two perspectives.
Negatively, they are noteworthy because they have so often been
cited as flagrant indications of psychic abnormality and thus
contribute to many misapprehensions of Ezekiel's prophetic function.
Positively, they may be seen as one of the most important aspects of
Ezekiel's self-representation, which is at one time both an accommodation to the old view of prophecy and a subtle adaptation to its new
medium.

The sign-actions have been a long-standing embarrassment within
the biblical tradition. The Talmud records a third-century incident:
'A heretic said to Rabbi Abbahu, "Your God is a joker; first he
commands to lie on the left side, then on the right side!"'[49]
Maimonides exclaims, 'God forbid to assume that God would make
his prophets appear an object of ridicule and sport in the eyes of the
ignorant, and order them to perform foolish acts',[50] and explains
them as purely visionary.

Fohrer's study has laid the grounds for the modern consensus that
prophetic sign-actions were actual, conscious events, in some cases
perhaps derived from ecstatic experience, but later developed into

public performances (Ezekiel's dumbness and lying on his side are cited as possible examples). Moreover, the purpose of these acts was fully in accord with the prophets' chief task of proclaiming the divine word in the most forceful way possible:

> They are means of public announcement. They ought to arouse curiosity, excite attention, and thereby also reach the unwilling, make the proclamation more expressive, cause a stir, act upon the imagination, and make the prophetic teaching more forceful.[51]

But the function of the sign-action is not, in Fohrer's view, exhausted by creating a public impression. It also has some causative bearing on the future, not directly, as in magic, but rather pointing to and giving assurance of the will and power of God. Lang underscores the first point but denies the second; public agitation is the only effect which the sign-actions are intended to have. 'They are rather to be regarded as a prototype of modern politically and socially agitating street theatre.'[52]

Yet the literal theory raises difficult problems when applied to exegesis of this book. First, in some cases such an interpretation either stretches the limits of credulity (the 430 days of bondage) or violates the logic of its context (the dumbness). Zimmerli suggests that in both these instances the literal sense originally intended has been obliterated by later development of the tradition (i.e., the placement of the dumbness in the call narrative and the vast extension of the period of bondage in accordance with the tradition about the duration of the Egyptian enslavement). Some interpreters (Cooke, Ewald) distinguish the genuine sign-actions from those which are probably or certainly imaginary, but their lists do not agree, and the test provides no grounds for such differentiation. Zimmerli refers to Ezekiel's conscious execution of some actions and unconscious experience of others (e.g., trembling, mute mourning),[53] but again, the distinction seems arbitrary.

No less troublesome is the question of whether the sign-actions are designed to make the kind of impression on viewers which both Fohrer and Lang attribute to them. Lying bound for more than a year is something entirely different from a street theatre production; the cost of such a lengthy 'performance' may be considered far in excess of its impact. Nor would the 'anti-sign' of not mourning his wife's death seem to have much theatrical value. Moreover, it is odd that there is so little indication of any public response to these actions. When we hear (through Ezekiel) of what the people think of him, it is striking that they only characterize him in terms of his *words*. He is a purveyor of YHWH's word (33.30), a sweet crooner (33.32), a master of rhetorical flourishes (21.5); but nowhere is he labelled as the extreme crank which anyone performing these weird antics would surely have appeared to the hard-nosed (3.7) exiles.

Finally, the question of actual performance is certainly muted in Ezekiel's representation, where emphasis falls entirely on the divine instruction[54] or, in the instance of the sign at the crossroads, quickly shifts from a vague command regarding the sign (21.24-25, in which it is completely unclear what is the medium for marking the roads, whether indeed this is anything other than a mental designation) to a description of the thing signified (21.26-28). Zimmerli considers this to be a weakening of the original form of the sign-action, so that it is wholly subordinated to the prophet's preaching. His comments (noted above) on how the dumbness and the lying bound have been 'developed' past the point of intelligibility suggest further that not only the speech form but the text itself has been marred or weakened by Ezekiel's followers, and perhaps even the prophet himself.

It would be preferable to assume that those who produced the present text did not bungle the job. A proper understanding of the sign-actions must take account both of their essential nature as communicative symbols and of the form in which they are reported, and I suggest that the two aspects are closely related. A remark made by Orelli is pertinent. Having observed the general disposition of the Israelites toward symbolical instruction and verification, he continues:

> But to Ezekiel in particular, who was cut off from the scene of the action and therefore not in the position to engage conspicuously in it, this symbolical acting, which made his listeners into viewers of the course of events willed by God, was especially natural. But also the above-mentioned even narrower restriction and confinement of his activity comes to expression in his symbolical representation.[55]

Orelli's crucial insight is to draw a connection between the sign-actions and the restriction of the prophet's public activity. In light of this connection, it is evident that interpretation of the sign-actions must be subsumed to a larger appreciation of Ezekiel's prophetic role. Orelli notes further that these actions have a bearing also upon the role of the audience, making them spectators as well as hearers. Although Orelli himself generally upholds a literal interpretation of the sign-actions, his comment encourages another possibility. It is difficult to see that their actual performance would be more compatible than oracular proclamation with limited public involvement. However, if Ezekiel is working in the first instance as a writer, then producing accounts of the sign-actions would be not only compatible with his mode of operation but also a significant enhancement of his presentation.

In order to understand why this should be the case, it is important to keep in mind the liminal position of early writers. Ong notes 'the difficulty that narrators long had in feeling themselves as other than oral performers'.[56] Accordingly, they provided their readers—or hearers at public readings—with means to orient themselves *vis-à-vis* (taking the term in an imaginative but not wholly figurative sense) the text. It is readily apparent how the sign-actions as a form of quasi-visual presentation could be instrumental in this process. Moreover, it is interesting that Ezekiel's vision accounts are always followed by references to these actions, so that one kind of 'visible narration' reinforces another.

Although less developed than the sign-actions, the expressive gestures which abound in the book may be understood in the same manner. Rather than a mark of Ezekiel's archaism (so Zimmerli[57]), they are a feature of the innovative form of his prophecy. They belong to the text of the message itself (6.11 subsumes the instruction to the messenger formula) and supply the supplemental information which written language requires, facilitating the audience's imaginative engagement with the inscribed word, perhaps even providing 'stage directions' for public readings.

But if Ezekiel's use of the sign-actions was motivated in part by the persistence of orality within the general ideology of communication, a much more important factor may be located within the ideology of prophecy. Prophets in Israel were well known for backing up their words with their bodies (e.g. 1 Kgs 22.11; 2 Kgs 13.14-19; Isa. 8.1-4; 20.2-4; Jer. 27.2; 28.10-11; 32.6-15[58]). Such sign-actions were perhaps valued as elements of personal style, as well as memorable dramatizations of a message. But more significantly, they were an assertion of the prophet's authority. The prophet so consumed with the divine word that finally his life (and even that of his family; cf. Isa. 8.18) was important only to illustrate it might well claim to speak for YHWH.

Respecting the significance of the sign-actions in delineating Ezekiel's prophetic function, it is not incidental that almost all of them appear within the first twenty-four chapters of the book. Cast in the role of narrator, Ezekiel speaks for God in commanding and interpreting the sign-actions as a vivid depiction of Israel's fate. But in representing his performance of them, Ezekiel shows his own profound and costly involvement in the people's suffering. 12.17-20 points to both aspects of the sign. The explanation given with the sign-action directs it outward as an illustration of the conditions imminent in beleaguered Jerusalem. But the sign also has an inner face: the figure rings with echoes of the prophetic tradition, especially Jer. 4.19-21, and thus testifies that this prophet, too, who is often thought to turn a dispassionate and even cruel eye toward his fellow Israelites,[59] feels their anguish in his own frame. Moreover, the fact that Ezekiel is enjoined to perform acts which are unnatural for any person (24.16), abhorrent to him as an observer of the law (4.14), and even in violation of the special restrictions laid upon him as a priest (shaving his hair) reinforces the claim asserted in the repeated messenger formula: this prophecy comes from YHWH. So far is it from being Ezekiel's own invention that he is even obliged to become alienated from his own identity in order to serve as its vehicle.

It is best to remain agnostic about whether any of the sign-actions was actually performed. One can only say that, while a number of them present great difficulties for a literal interpretation, they are all comprehensible and effective as literary devices. Gunkel saw in Ezekiel a genuinely ecstatic personality quite unlike Isaiah and Jeremiah, who imitated ecstatic behavior with calculated effect.[60] It is probable that Gunkel underestimated Ezekiel's subtlety. What we see in his sign-actions is a highly conscious self-representation, a literary effort which is calculated in the best sense: one so finely coordinated and attuned to his audience's perception of reality that the imitation of an action is more persuasive than action itself.

## Chapter 4

## MAKING AN AUDIENCE

אין דורשין...במרכבה ביחיד אלא אם כן היה חכם ומבין מדעתו

No one may expound the Merkavah even to a single individual, unless to one who is already astute and understands it out of personal experience (*Mishnah Ḥagigah* 2.1).

To believe that your impressions hold good for others is to be released from the cramp and confinement of personality (Virginia Woolf, *The Common Reader*).

More than with any other prophet, the identity of Ezekiel's audience has been debated. The question has arisen repeatedly, if somewhat obliquely, as an aspect of the attempt to fix the geographic limits of the prophet's activity. Answers to the question have generally been rendered in static terms. That is, one assumes that those addressed were already constituted as an historically determinate group (viz., Jerusalemites or exiles) which can be identified on grounds wholly independent of Ezekiel's relation to them. But his status as a writer calls this assumption into question. For there is a sense in which the writer has no ready-made audience. It has been seen that writing requires some degree of social withdrawal; the author must be alone in order to reflect and create. And central to that creative process is an imaginative evocation of the public whom one wishes to reach. The writer mentally calls forth an audience and then devises structural means by which their attention can be engaged. In this way the text itself becomes the instrument whereby the audience— drawn theoretically from all potential readers and hearers—is constituted. The author's task, then, is not so much to address a previously identifiable social group as to create a new community. Booth describes the process thus:

> The author makes his readers. If he makes them badly—that is, if he simply waits, in all purity, for the occasional reader whose

perceptions and norms happen to match his own, then his conception must be lofty indeed if we are to forgive him for his bad craftsmanship. But if he makes them well—that is, makes them see what they have never seen before, moves them into a new order of perception and experience altogether—he finds his reward in the peers he has created.[1]

Creation of the intended audience represents one of the greatest challenges in the move from live speech to writing. It may be seen as the obverse of the difficulty experienced by early writers in establishing their own identity as distinct from that of oral performers. While the notion of the 'implied/ideal/mock reader' has recently received much attention from literary critics, its historical aspect warrants further investigation. It is likely that biblical scholars are among those who would benefit most from a careful attempt to trace how writers have adapted oral speech forms to audiences who are in the first instance present only in their imaginations. (The possibility, which must be reckoned with in the case of Ezekiel, of a writer reading or reciting prepared works to a live audience does not represent an exception, for the writer was alone at the time of composition.) The two problems—first, of finding a proper authorial stance, and second, of inventing an audience—belong together as aspects of a communications situation in which the partners do not confront one another directly, and the shape of the text may in various ways reflect attempts to solve one or both of these problems.

The writer must not just help the audience adjust to the new and often heavy demands for comprehension which a previously composed text presents, but also stimulate them to make the effort. They must be moved to care about the work itself, usually in the absence of its creator, and without any opportunity to respond directly, or at least verbally. There is a certain paradoxical character to the techniques which the writer employs in order to fulfill this task. As previously noted, written language generally relies upon explicit syntactical and lexical features to a greater degree than does live speech, where the speaker's presence contributes much to its clarity. But on the other hand, as Iser has shown, it is precisely by means of its indeterminacies and unformulated connections that a literary text engages its readers. In the process of supplying its logical gaps, they contribute something of themselves to the text, and thus it assumes significance for them: 'For we generally tend to regard something we have made ourselves as being real. And so it can be said that indeterminacy is the fundamental precondition for reader participation.'[2] The writer's responsibility, then, is to establish the conditions for a collaborative relationship with the audience, giving readers or hearers sufficient purchase on the text so that they can in turn exercise their creative responsibility in producing a coherent and (to some degree) personal reading.

Texts differ in the level at which this collaboration is sought. Of course, for the work to be meaningful at all, author and audience must share some frame of reference and range of interests. But eliciting appreciation of a pun, a joke, or a literary allusion is a much less ambitious undertaking than seeking collaboration in a question of moral judgment. In the former case, a common linguistic and cultural background is sufficient basis for appreciation of the work. In the latter, it is important that the audience also regard the author—though perhaps little known as a personal figure—as one qualified to speak on questions of behavior and of values. The author must, in short, be viewed as an authority, if we are to allow ourselves not merely to be entertained but indeed persuaded in matters of consequence.

It is evident that the collaboration which Ezekiel requires is of no casual sort. The prophet of exile is commissioned to move the stricken people out of a posture of defiant confidence (11.3; 12.17) or self-pity (18.2, 25) and into one of self-recognition. In the idiom of his prophecy, he is to 'make known to/tell (הודע/הגד) Israel its abominations' (16.2; 20.4; 22.2; 23.36). Ezekiel subjects his audience to the most stringent test of moral maturity: whether they can be brought to pass judgment on themselves. And this demand is connected throughout with another one, that of recognizing YHWH as the sole source of both blessing and judgment. Being like the nations, worshipping gods of wood and stone, is not an option for Israel (20.32). Desired or not, the relationship with God is exclusive and inalienable. The goal of Ezekiel's prophecy is an epistemic one, expressed in the constantly repeated recognition formula, וידעתם/וידע כי אני יי ('and you/they shall know that I am YHWH'); and that recognition constitutes both the basis of Israel's self-knowledge, and also the fundamental condition of the nation's existence.

It should not be surprising to find that, where the project on which author and audience must collaborate is of profound, even ultimate consequence, the structural means for eliciting such collaboration become complex. It is the purpose of this chapter to show that this is indeed the case with Ezekiel and to consider the devices he employs, first, for engaging his audience's attention and active involvement and, second, for establishing his own authority to speak. This investigation is concerned with the pragmatics of communication, the way in which the relationship between the partners of discourse is stylistically established or elucidated, and only secondarily with the actual content conveyed.

The narrative analysis of Labov and Waletzky is useful in highlighting the pragmatic aspect of narrative style. Among the components of 'natural narrative' (i.e., that which is told in everyday life, usually out of personal experience and without rehearsal), they include 'evaluation': 'that part of the narrative which reveals the attitude of the narrator towards the narrative by emphasizing the relative importance of some narrative units as compared to others'.[3] Extending application of the term to narrative literature, Pratt suggests that evaluative devices constitute a secondary structure running throughout the work and, in addition to indicating the narrator's attitude, they are aimed at informing the audience's perspective and assuring them of the significance of the story. Evaluative devices are of various sorts. They may appear lexically, as intensifiers, qualifiers, or comparators; or semantically, as direct narrative statements either within ('And I said to myself. . . ') or outside ('It was a strange experience') the story proper. They may be formally defined, as complex auxiliary statements, subordinate clauses, or repetitions which slow the pace of narration. Or they may draw their significance from the cultural context, such as citation of authoritative persons or texts, or reference to commonly understood symbolic actions ('I cross myself'). Thus it is evident that, while evaluative structures reflect literary conventions, an equally or more important factor is the particular cultural tradition within which they are to be interpreted. Moreover, as well as guiding the reader's response to the text, they show how the narrative is related to a larger world of experience and thought.

I have already argued that Ezekiel's first-person narrative yields little information about the prophet as an individual. Yet, when examined as a source of evaluative statements, the same spare frame is surprisingly fruitful. If, indeed, Ezekiel remains hidden as a personality, nonetheless he emerges quite distinctly as a resourceful discourse partner who punctuates his account with markers to direct the audience's attention and understanding. Some of the prominent (and from the perspective of traditional biblical criticism, troublesome) formal features of the book seem to function in precisely this way.

### Establishing a Partnership

One need not go beyond the first verse to find the distinctiveness, and also the difficulty, of Ezekiel's style. Alone among all the prophetic books, this one begins, not with a titular formula referring to the prophet in the third person but with the prophet's own first-person narrative. Yet it could hardly be called a proper self-introduction, for the verse does not even include the prophet's name.[4] More than that, the initial term by which Ezekiel sets the scene is radically peculiar: 'the thirtieth year' has no analogue, either in the rest of the book or in Scripture as a whole. Many attempts have been made to identify the era to which the date belongs.[5] The Targum and the Mekilta set the example for much Jewish exegesis in reckoning from Hilkiah's discovery of the scroll during Josiah's reign, thus arriving at a date of 593/92 (which accords with 1.2). Lindblom is among the commentators who have suggested that the thirtieth year refers to the prophet's age; James Smith, identifying Ezekiel as a prophet of the Northern Kingdom, thinks the allusion is to the fall of Samaria. Torrey considers it 'obvious and certain' that the reference is to Manasseh's regnal period and (most improbably) cites this contradiction of the dominant time frame as the reason the first chapter was for some time put under rabbinic ban.

Spiegel regards as hopelessly speculative all attempts to identify a special era for the verse. Instead, he posits a separate oracle, dated to the thirtieth year of the exile, which possibly referred to a vision of God withdrawing to the heavens after the destruction of the Temple. While 'the rabbis could not include in the approved Scriptures for school and synagogue a chapter upon which an entire system of occult lore was based', neither could they wholly erase the memory of an ancient prophecy. He concludes:

> The course wisely adopted was to leave some trace of the withdrawn chapter, a mark for the initiated that something had been omitted here to be confided orally to the choicest few, while

disclosing to the general reader a summary indication of the content dealt with. . . .[6]

Spiegel's supposition also can be criticized as highly speculative, and it fails to acknowledge that what the rabbis left in was sufficient basis for the occult. Nonetheless, it does raise an interesting possibility: namely, that the reference to the thirtieth year is *deliberately* elliptical. Whether the nature of that ellipsis is historical (positing reference to a separate time frame) or literary (assuming a lost oracle), considering its effect may well be more fruitful than attempting to supply the lack. Spiegel's comment is helpful in turning the discussion of the thirtieth year away from the missing referent itself and raising the very different question of how the ellipsis functions with respect to the reader. I would suggest that it is only from that perspective that something definite can be said.

The very lack of information in this first verse testifies to a certain kind of relationshp between the discourse partners. There is no need for this writer to give his name or specify the chronological allusion, for he is addressing familiars. Ezekiel uses the restricted linguistic code of those who share a common experience and frame of reference, the language of an in-group. Whatever the thirtieth year may have meant, Ezekiel expects his readers to know without being told. Such abbreviated language is customary in a conversation or a personal letter; but when it appears in a formal discourse situation, and especially one as tightly controlled as this, some explanation is surely required.

Any restricted code functions in two ways. First, the code builds a sense of comradeship between speaker and addressee and thus evokes a certain kind of response. It is gratifying to have one's understanding acknowledged; there is a natural desire to show oneself worthy of the trust implied by attending closely to the communication. Moreover, our sympathies become engaged along with our intellects; we are more inclined to accept what is said because of the intimate tone in which it is conveyed. But the other face of intimacy is exclusion, and that is the second function of a restricted linguistic code. It emphasizes the fact that the message is not intended for everyone, those who cannot use the code are meant to remain on the outside.

Not all usages of a restricted code are, of course, equally exclusive. When referring to widely known phenomena, one may exploit the advantage of apparent intimacy without actually reducing the potential audience. Since the historical referent for 'the thirtieth year' has been lost since antiquity, it is not possible to judge how exclusionary this ellipsis was for Ezekiel's contemporaries, i.e., whether the unspecified era was common currency among the exiles, or whether the allusion might indeed have been clear to only the relatively few who had personal contact with or knowledge of the prophet.[7] However, I think the implication of the second possibility must be considered: that, with the very first phrase, Ezekiel's text begins to select its audience, sets a test by which they may identify themselves as those privileged and qualified to hear this prophecy.

The text does in several places seem to evidence an awareness of some sub-group among the exiles. In 5.3-4, within the image of the shaved hair, weighed and allotted to various forms of destruction, the prophet is commanded to take out a few hairs and tuck them into his sleeves, and from these to take a few again and toss them into the fire. The image is never expounded in the interpretation section, and so its enigmas remain. On what basis are these few saved out: as a reward for righteousness, or in order to bear witness in some way (cf. 6.8-10; 12.16; 14.22-23)? What is the nature and purpose of the second burning: a further purging (cf. 20.33-38) by punishing fire, or is this perhaps a martyrs' death, by which other Israelites are both judged and redeemed?[8]

A distinction among the exiles is also implied by God's avowal within the denunciation of the deceiving prophets that '(they) will neither be included in the council of my people nor written in the register of the House of Israel nor come (back) to the land of Israel' (13.9). The phrase בסוד עמי ('in the council of my people') recalls Jeremiah's references to סוד יי ('the council of YHWH', Jer. 23.18, 22) as the place where genuine prophets are groomed for the task (cf. 1 Kgs 22.19-23). Yet the change which Ezekiel works on the phrase yields a reference, not to the ultimate source of the prophets' words (although this, too, is his concern), but to their place within the community of survivors. The notion of a register (כתב) that reflects discriminatory decisions indicates that the circle of the reconstituted Israel will be, in comparison to the pre-exilic population, a contracted one, and not only due to the depredations of the Babylonians.

Again, in the final section of the Oholah-Oholibah allegory, the

prerogative of rendering judgment is granted to some (otherwise
unspecified) group of 'righteous men' (23.45). Zimmerli may well be
right to see this whole section (vv. 36-49) as comprising 'didactic
example stories' removed in both spirit and time from the genuine
prophetic word.[9] But it is noteworthy that within the period of the
text's formation, a notion of a group in some way distinct from the
other survivors[10] was finding at least one locus of its development in
the prophecy of Ezekiel.[11]

The particular points at which Ezekiel makes use of a noticeably
restricted code give further evidence that it is a deliberate rhetorical
device. The intimacy indicated by the first verse immediately
disposes readers to identify themselves with Ezekiel. That this is at
the same time identifying themselves over against the deliberately
deaf majority (3.5-7) is shown by repeated use throughout the call of
emphatically exclusive third-person references to the Israelites:
בית מרי המה ('*they* are a rebellious house', 2.5, 6, 7; 3.9, 26, 27; cf. 2.8;
3.7). Two other terms which appear much later in the narrative
frame emphasize Ezekiel's intimacy with his audience. These are
לגלותנו ('[reckoned according] to our exile', 33.21; 40.1), whereby
Ezekiel stresses the unity of experience and therefore also of
perspective between the audience and himself, and the unspecified
שמה ('there', 40.1), whose effect is similar to that noted for the
thirtieth year. These occur at key junctures, first when news of
Jerusalem's fall reaches Babylon and the prophet's mouth is opened,
and then at the beginning of Ezekiel's greatest restoration vision. At
these two turning points, which constitute on the one hand a
definitive break with the past and on the other a bold delineation of
the future, Ezekiel takes pains to assure his audience that the
message is addressed to them, the select group to whom, by virtue of
their special relation with the prophet (cf. 5.3),[12] the word of new
hope is meaningful.

But the assumption of a personal relationship between writer and
audience contains an element of risk. The danger is that subjectivity
will prove more suspect than attractive, that the writer who dares to
speak in a personal voice and to presume commonality with readers
will not be recognized as an authority figure.[13] Being (as the last
chapter showed) acutely aware of the threat to his prophetic
authority posed by the external situation, it is likely that Ezekiel was
aware also of this danger inherent in his style. If, then, he chose for

his prophecy a literary form which lays a personal claim upon the reader, he did not press that advantage too far. Rather he balanced the eye-witness account, glimmering with a few moments of confidentiality, with another technique, one which is the dominant and most distinctive feature of Ezekiel's style.

Ezekiel effects a radical transformation in the ordinary forms of prophetic discourse by casting them in the form of divine speech. Whereas Jeremiah raises a strident lament over the people's jibes at his predictions of doom (Jer. 17.14-18), the same situation is represented in Ezekiel as God's announcement *to* the prophet (33.30-33), however gratuitous that might seem. Zimmerli considers this alienation of the prophetic lament as 'one of the principal form-critical problems of Ezekiel's oracles'.[14] It is indeed unlikely that the development can be explained in form-critical terms, i.e., construed on the model of conventional oral speech. But when viewed from a functional perspective, as an accommodation to written communication, the all-absorptive character of the divine speech appears less as a problem than as a solution. It is one way of coming to terms with the difficulty of finding an authorial stance and therefore corresponds closely to the problem of creating and situating the audience.

In order to appreciate the difficulty which early writers faced, it is necessary to consider how their situation differed from that of traditional oral narrators. The oral poet's relation to the literary culture is one of full rapport. Though not wholly submerged, the individual's talent and imagination are submitted to the service of the tradition. The oral poet does not pose as an eye-witness but rather takes the viewpoint of an ominiscient external narrator whose authority and reliability are unquestionable. It is finally the anonymous tradition itself which tells the tale. But the move to non-traditional written composition greatly facilitates the growth of authorial self-awareness, and with it a change in narrative style. In addition to finding ways to 'imply' the audience, the tellers of written tales must also make decisions about their own implication, i.e., the imaginative representation of themselves as narrators within the work. A comparison of the first lines of the *Iliad* ('Sing, goddess, the anger of Peleus' son Achilleus and its devastation') and of the *Aeneid* ('I sing of arms and of men') shows a significant development in authorial consciousness.[15] If, as seems probable, Homer utilized writing in his work of consolidating, refining, and perhaps also developing a critical perspective on the epic tradition,[16] then his invocation of the Muse (which is not a regular feature of oral epic) may well be an attempt to mark this version as 'authorized', while reducing his own role to that of providing the occasion for her song. Some seven centuries later, Vergil boldly claims the epic as his creation and yet still authoritative, a newly made fundament of the tradition of Augustan Rome.

Ezekiel takes on the issue of narrative stance more directly than any other prophet. Here there are none of the problems which make formal analysis of the prophetic books such a slippery business: ummarked blendings of divine and human speech, stylistic shifts, ambiguous self-reference or failure to identify those addressed. All discourse in Ezekiel is clearly marked with respect to speaker and addressee, as well as being rendered from a consistent perspective. And that perspective is distinctly a literary one. Even Zimmerli, who measures the text always against the categories established by form criticism, can on the question of setting do no more than raise compositional and editorial issues. The shape of the text itself frustrates attempts to formulate oral settings. While other prophets appear to us as before an audience, often prefacing their speeches with a public summons (שמעו, האזינו, הקשיבו 'hear', 'give ear', 'attend'), the imperative which dominates this book—הנבא ('prophesy')— is addressed to the prophet alone. Never do we see Ezekiel fulfilling that commission in the manner of the classical prophet; he speaks only as narrator, only within the confines of the text. Yet it could hardly be said that the prophet asserts an *authorial* consciousness: his writing activity is represented as no more than recording in response to explicit divine commands (24.2; 43.11). Ezekiel claims to be the privileged first listener to God's speech, passing on everything exactly as he received it from God.[17] The classificatory appellation בן אדם ('human being'), which so frequently opens the divine addresses, is deliberately inglorious, marking Ezekiel's status as the recipient, not the source, of the authoritative word.

It is self-evident that in phrasing all—not only the prophetic message proper but even description of his own situation—as divine speech addressed to himself, Ezekiel is invoking the highest authority for his prophecy. It could, in fact, be said that in this absorptive divine discourse he has found the ultimate archival form. The essential quality of archival speech is that it preserves an utterance by dissociating it from a particular speaker or context of production. Furthermore, the utterance gains authority by being embedded in a context—traditional, historical, or ritualistic—where it appears in some way fundamental to the life of the community. When, in addition, a transcendent source is specifically invoked, the archived discourse becomes highly resistant, if not impervious, to criticism. Called to speak in circumstances which he (correctly) perceived to be inhospitable to the exercise of his prophetic authority,[18] Ezekiel devises the extraordinary means of refracting his speech wholly through the medium of divine discourse. Thus he magnifies greatly the features already described as characteristic of written discourse: viz., the text's relative autonomy from its author and the original context of production, as well as the unequal distribution of power in a one-way communications situation.

By portraying himself as a listener rather than an initiator of speech, Ezekiel also claims another advantage. Through representation of his own impressions and behavior, he shows how hearers of God's word are to understand it and respond. The inaugural vision and call narrative are well-marked with evaluative elements to guide those who would align themselves with Ezekiel rather than with the heedless and rebellious majority. They testify to his awe at the vision he is granted (הנורא 'awesome', 1.22; possibly the difficult ויראה להם 'and they were dreadful [?]', 1.18; ואפל על-פני 'and I fell on my face', 1.28), and then shortly to his distress at the task he must assume (ואלך מר בחמת רוחי ויד-יי עלי חזקה 'and I went, bitter, in a raging spirit, while the hand of YHWH was firm upon me', 3.14; ואשב שם שבעת ימים משמים בתוכם 'and I sat there for seven days, desolate in their midst', 3.15). Repeatedly we are reminded that Ezekiel is the unwilling vehicle, not the source, of this message. A variant mode of introducing evaluative comments into the narrative report is used in the second divine vision, when the divine guide tells Ezekiel how to judge (תועבות גדלות/רעות 'great/wicked abominations', 8.6, 9, 13, 15) what he is about to see in the Temple.

This evaluative structure clarifies the double sense in which Ezekiel functions as a divinely engineered 'display' (מופת) to Israel. First and most overtly, he is a portent, a living image of God's judgment and the people's fate (12.6, 11; 24.24). But as much as he is a warning sign, Ezekiel is also a guide: a model of the human creature who *does* hear the divine word, who responds fully and appropriately to what YHWH is doing (24.27). Displaying that model is the purpose of the first-person narrative frame.

Though not directly connected with his self-representation, one other feature of Ezekiel's narrative style figures importantly in the evaluative structure he establishes for his readers. It would seem to be one of his least felicitous effects to have peppered the divine visions so liberally with qualifiers and comparators: the constantly repeated כעין (1.4, 7, 16, 22, 27; 10.9), דמות (1.5, 10, 13, 22, 26, 28; 10.1, 10, 21, 22), -כ (1.13, 24; 10.1), כמראה (1.13; 26, 27, 28; 10.1), מראה (1.5, 13, 16, 28; 10.9, 10, 22). Widengren took these to indicate the abstruse character of Ezekiel's visions, involving such dreamlike features as loose association of events, shifting images, vagueness of setting, and inclusion of knowledge extraneous to the visionary experience itself. Interestingly, he saw them also as indications of the role which writing played in the prophetic process:

> This kind of visions must have been difficult for the prophet to render adequately when he wishes to communicate his experiences. The numerous uncertainties, the many 'like the image of' testify to his struggle with the contents of the vision. It is for this reason quite impossible to think that he would have been able to retain such a turbulent as well as vague scenery as that of Chapter 1 without any conscious literary effort. Conceivably, the comparisons must in at least some cases have been the result of his elaboration of the vision when committing it to paper.[19]

While I agree that the terms of Ezekiel's representation are indeed features of written discourse, suggesting 'a rather considerable distance between the original experience and its reflecting in the committing to paper',[20] it is not clear that his struggle was primarily to cope with the complexity of the visions. Certainly this prophet above all others was capable of dealing with fluid images without falling into the kind of awkwardness evidenced here. Yet there is something about the content of these visions which could legitimately make Ezekiel nervous. They are visions of the divine glory itself; they represent his deepest penetration into the mystery of God. It is not surprising that Ezekiel's concern for the correct understanding of his message should manifest itself with particular acuteness at this point.

The qualifiers and the explicit comparators show Ezekiel to be conscientious to the point of tedium in marking his speech here as non-literal. It is a mark of his self-awareness as an authoritative speaker, as well as the sensitivity of his subject, that Ezekiel provides unmistakable internal guards against misreading his vision reports. In order to understand Ezekiel's anxiety on this point, it is useful to recall the background against which he limns his account. On one side, he defends the seriousness and integrity of metaphorical language against those who see only its ornamental aspect (the criticism implicit in 21.5; cf. 33.30-33). Rhetorical flourishes play no part in Ezekiel's report of the most exalted of his visions. What is everywhere apparent is the way he limits his own power of imaginative expression for the sake of accuracy. Thus Ezekiel asserts the legitimacy of metaphorical speech to describe, albeit neither exhaustively nor precisely, realities which can be expressed in no other way.

But probably the greater danger against which he guards is that figurative speech will be used and taken too seriously, namely, as a means of domesticating the heavenly sphere. Within Israel, Ezekiel competes with those who spin so-called 'visions' out of their own imaginations (13.3-7). Moreover, on all sides Israel is pressed by or scattered among nations which make no distinction between human claims and divine authority. The explosion of religio-political myth as a form of authoritative speech is, of course, a key strategy in his oracles against the nations (27.3; 28.2; 29.3). The aim of Ezekiel's meticulously qualified speech is to insure that the heavenly realities will be illumined by rather than identified with the objects of comparison drawn from the human world. But so careful is he to distinguish himself from those who mislead the people with illegitimate use of language, that he produces what amounts to a caricature of genuine prophetic discourse. The almost painful self-consciousness which produced this deformation is hardly conceivable except as belonging to a writer.

## Establishing the Opposition

If it is possible to discern subtle means whereby Ezekiel establishes a partnership with those whom he addresses, the book also delineates, in a far more obvious way, another kind of relationship. Though a series of quotations, Ezekiel characterizes the attitudes prevalent among his contemporaries. This is how Ezekiel summons and confronts his opposition. Again, as with the sign-actions and the figure of Ezekiel's dumbness, there seems to be a connection between use of the rhetorical device and the structure of the book as a whole. In the pre-fall section of the book, the citations of Israelite speech are adduced always in a directly adversarial sense; on the point of and after the collapse (33.10 and 37.11 respectively), the people's expressions of despair appear not so much wrong-headed as inadequate to reckon with the surprising action of God.

The quotations of popular speech have been taken to afford direct evidence of Ezekiel's interaction with his environment. Zimmerli comments on the vitality which they lend to the prophetic message, locating it in 'a process of real encounter with the men of Israel to whom the prophet was sent'.[21] Greenberg agrees that the quotations are the only substantial information we are given regarding Ezekiel's social environment and asserts further that they are 'for the most part a provocation to the word of YHWH, in the sense that the prophet meditated on them until they became cornerstones of (his) prophecy'.[22] Yet one may ask whether these scholars have not mistaken a technique of vivid style for a direct reflection of the external situation. While it is surely correct that the quotations are significant in connection with the circumstances of Ezekiel's prophesying, the following discussion will show how an accurate estimation of their function and value must be rendered in terms of the particular mode of this prophecy.

The first fact to be noted with respect to the quotations is that, like all other speech in the book, they are incorporated within a one-sided narrative dominated by God's voice. We do not witness a direct confrontation between the prophet and another party, such as is common in other prophetic writings (e.g., between Amos and Amaziah, Isaiah and Hezekiah, or Jeremiah and Pashur). The words of Ezekiel's contemporaries are audible only after they have passed through the double filter of prophetic and divine speech. The result is something very far from conversational rhetoric, modelled on natural (non-literary) language. What we hear is rather a complex orchestration of voices within voices which depends for its coherence and effectiveness on tight narrative control—precisely the kind of control which writing allows. That Ezekiel is able to sustain this complex echoing throughout the book is a mark not only of his exceptional skill,[23] but also of the literary medium he utilizes.

Writing facilitates the move from natural language to stylized usages by the distance it introduces between the author and the represented speech acts. These speech acts can be manipulated and brought into interaction in ways not possible with oral narration. Through the coordination of diverse voices and perspectives within a single work, writers are able to achieve more complex effects in point of view, which, as Scholes and Kellogg observe, is one of the most significant developmental processes in literary history.[24]

A second and related point: if, as Greenberg thinks, the quotations did once serve as stimuli for Ezekiel's meditation and prophecy, what is now much more evident is that they have been shaped for presentation under pressure of the book's theocentric perspective. The shift from dialogue to this kind of refracted speech involves an alienation even more radical than that which Zimmerli noted concerning absorption of prophetic speech forms into divine speech. The statements of the Israelites have been removed from their original contexts and subordinated to divine discourse, and in the process, the boundaries of the reported speech have been weakened. They are now permeable to new intentions which challenge or mock the views of those to whom the speech is attributed. Sometimes the context of prophetic/divine speech imposes itself upon the quotation to the point of distortion. The optimistic attempt to make peace with the conditions of exile—נהיה כגוים כמשפחות הארצות ('Let us be like the families of the [other] lands', 20.32)—is thus twisted into a statement of blatant stupidity by the addition, לשרת עץ ואבן ('serving wood and stone'). But, though unrealistic at the literal level, the parody is deadly accurate in exposing the godless defiance latent in the original expression.

Third, it is important to recognize that point-of-view is bound in the closest way with the process of speech reception. The significance of the shift from dialogical representation to the stylization of reported speech must be understood in this light. Direct dialogue includes no direct grammatical connections between statements of different discourse partners; generally no clues are given beyond the words exchanged for how various viewpoints and speakers are to be assessed. A unified context of discourse, on the other hand, serves as an evaluative structure directed at readers. Ezekiel resolves the multifariousness characteristic of live encounter into a single perspective; the authority of divine speech now tells us how to judge these subordinated speech acts. In the disputation- or discussion-oracle (e.g. ch. 18; 20.32-44; 33.11-20),[25] he seems to have created a formal structure particularly suited for directing the battle of opposed verbal forces. But it is evident, especially in the most developed of these, ch. 18, how far this prophet is removed from the give and take of direct confrontation. Like a medieval schoolman, he establishes an agonistic frame for his carefully developed analytic discourse. The encounter with the opponent is a literary convention, and a fitting one in a society still oriented to oral argumentation in education and public affairs.[26] But it is precisely as a literary convention chosen by the author that the opponent's speech must be recognized as a secondary phenomenon rather than (as Greenberg suggests) an immediate stimulus for or determinant of the discourse.

Fourth and finally, it is important for understanding the way the quotations function that they are often styled and sometimes specifically named as traditional sayings or proverbs, משלים (12.22; cf. 12.23; 16.44; 18.2). Despite their apparent simplicity, proverbs are a linguistic form of considerable power and social complexity. Their power derives from the fact that these anonymous sayings are backed by the weight of numbers and tradition. Proverbs are a popular, oral form of archival speech; because they articulate both the present consensus of the community and 'the wisdom of all the ancients' (Sir. 39.1), it is particularly difficult to refute the values they express. The cultural status of proverbs is further specified by the fact that they belong to 'the working class of metaphorical language',[27] using imagery drawn from common features of the social and natural environment. They are not in the first instance a literary device wielded by the few privileged creators of high culture; their primary sphere is rather ordinary conversation, where they provide flashes of insight into events of everyday life.

It does not follow, however, that proverbially based speech is pedestrian or transparent. Rather, the very simplicity of the form entails difficulties in at least two respects. First, the brevity of proverbs means that they offer few internal clues to interpretation. Both imagery and grammatical structure are generally elliptical and therefore presuppose a shared cultural background between the user and the hearer of the proverb. Some traditional sayings are more than elliptical; they in fact defy comprehension when construed in ordinary linguistic or logical terms. The best example I know is an expression used in the Southern United States to indicate that something is indisputably true: 'Does a chicken have lips?' (its use being comparable to more common and obvious expressions such as 'Is there sand on the beach? Is the Pope Catholic?'). One has to know that the assumed answer (although contrary to ordinary experience) is 'yes' in order to understand the point being made. Proverbial speech, then, is deeply embedded in the usages of particular cultures. The lack of internal specification must be supported by a broad base of common knowledge and linguistic conventions (which may, as in this case, override experiential knowledge) within the community of proverb users and hearers. It is a 'hot' (i.e., highly interactive) kind of discourse:

> The hearer... is forced to 'process' what has been heard and supply the missing elements to obtain an intelligible grasp of the content which is being conveyed. . . . The use of a saying challenges the receiver to break the cultural and linguistic code of the form, release its semantic content, and supply its immediate contextual referents.[28]

The second complication associated with the form of the proverb involves discerning its proper relation to the situation of usage. The proverb's spareness renders it adaptable to many different contexts in which it may function quite variously. Seitel cites as such an instance the Ibo (East Nigerian) proverb, 'A baby on its mother's back does not know the way is long'. When spoken by a priestess to a young girl before they set off on the long journey to an oracular cave,[29] it is an expression of comfort; uttered in reference to a spendthrift child, it criticizes one who benefits heedlessly from others' labors. On the other hand, a single tradition may often preserve two contradictory proverbs which would seem to suit identical situations (e.g. Prov. 26.4 and 26.5). The impact of this linguistic form rests wholly on the speaker's ability to infer a fit between a few familiar words and the present context, in all its singularity and complexity. Again, such an ability involves not only an accurate assessment of the situation but also familiarity with the hearers, so that they can be touched and moved by the sounding of even a brief note.

The above remarks indicate that proverb usage is a very socially sensitive activity, whose effectiveness depends upon the previous existence of a well-articulated frame of reference common to speaker and hearer, as well as acute perception of the immediate conditions for reception. Implicit in this, although it is generally (and perhaps deliberately) not apparent, is that proverbs serve their essential function in the management of conflict. Traditional sayings are generated and perpetuated by the existence of recurrent tensions in personal and social life. They mediate the conflict by projecting it onto the plane of metaphorical speech, where it can be construed in impersonal terms and resolved, at least temporarily, through the evocation of anonymous, seemingly objective wisdom.

It is evident from enumeration of these features how Ezekiel's grounding of his dispute with the people in citation of proverbial speech is both deliberate and impressive. Thus he focuses his attack directly on the heart of the tradition whose distortions it is his charge to expose. Ezekiel opposes anonymous (in this case, insidiously so) popular wisdom with the much more powerful authority, repeatedly and unambiguously identified, of divine speech. Further, he asserts his own position within the community by showing himself master of its code. Ezekiel fights archival speech with archival speech, turning pithy sayings back on their speakers (18.25), replacing corrupt proverbs with new ones which accurately represent the power of God and, moreover, validate his own position (12.22-23). He even dares to formulate 'traditional sayings' out of intentions which were never articulated publicly or indeed brought to full consciousness among the Israelites (11.3; 20.32).[30]

Equally important as the traditional nature of proverbial speech for understanding Ezekiel's usage is its character as interactive discourse. Fontaine's comment (cited above) on the way that the hearer is challenged to break the cultural and linguistic code in which the saying is couched in order to release its meaning is strongly reminiscent of what Iser has said about the reader's task being to fill in the gaps of the text. The two types of interaction are combined in the prophet's usage, so that the text becomes the context whereby the proverb is interpreted and, on the other hand, the proverb crystallizes certain insights which deepen understanding of the text.

The clearest instance of such mutual interpretation is seen in ch. 16. כאמה בתה ('Like mother, like daughter', 16.44), the only proverb placed in the mouth of non-Israelites (and, accordingly, the only one which Ezekiel cites with approval) demands explication in an immediate sense, because of its highly elliptical form. The next verse spells out the point of comparison between the two women, yet it remains unintelligible in terms of the popular belief in the special status that attaches to Jerusalem as David's city. In order to make sense of the proverb, Ezekiel's audience is forced out of their ordinary way of thinking and back to acceptance of the unflattering pedigree asserted at the beginning of the counter-history (16.3). But the narrative is at the same time amplified by the proverb, for it forces the audience to imagine even more than the prophet reports: that the Hittite mother, too, was scandalous, and so Jerusalem is damned by bloodline as well as by behavior.

A more complex kind of reinforcement between the proverb and the larger text is seen in connection with the most enigmatic of the proverbial sayings: לא בקרוב בנות בתים היא הסיר ואנחנו הבשר (11.3). Since this seems to represent Ezekiel's own formulation of the popular sentiment rather than a genuine saying (cf. 11.5), it may have puzzled his contemporaries no less than later commentators. The general purport of the first clause would appear to be that this is not a time for construction.[31] What is not clear is whether the expression conveys the complacency of the *nouveaux riches*, who have taken over the houses of the exiles ('No immediate need to build. . . '), or the urgency of the besieged ('No time now. . . '). The same ambiguity is present in the second clause: does the pot image capture the smug self-consciousness of those who feel themselves to be choice morsels, the newly elect of the secure city, or the less sanguine expectation that, although the enemy may press hotly around them, Jerusalem's inhabitants will at least be spared the worst fate of falling into fiery destruction? In either case, the pot image seems at first to express a sense of relative safety, but the prophet gives it another cast entirely in the context of God's reply (11.6-7). Here the sinister aspect inherent in the figure (cf. Mic. 3.3) comes to the fore: Jerusalem is filled, not with the select and safe, but with the slain, victims of their own corrupt leaders (cf. 9.9; 22.2-3; 34.17-21), who will themselves be tossed out to the doubtful mercy of strangers (11.9, where the pot figure is abandoned in favor of clear reference to war and exile).

The saying in 11.3 is enriched by the very different kind of משל in 24.3-12, which achieves two transformations on the theme of the pot. There (with the fall of the city imminent, cf. 24.16) we actually see the caldron set on the fire which hovers in the background of ch. 11, and the choice cuts boiled, cooked through, and emptied out. With a change in emphasis from contents to container, it then becomes clear how from affording protection is the pot—filth- (or 'rust-', חלאה, 24.6, 11, 12) filled, boiled dry, and finally melted in the blaze (cf. 22.18). Ezekiel's fluid symbol system allows the figure to gather into itself other images of what is happening within the city: most notably, the dross melted in the furnace (22.18-22), but also perhaps that of intergenerational cannibalism (5.10; cf. 36.13; the references to bloodshed [24.6-9], though not thoroughly integrated into the figure, promote this association). The result is a multi-dimensional picture of corruption and internal violence so shocking that God's judgment (11.11) must be taken as a matter of course. Yet presentation of the pot image as a popular saying (11.3) also contributes something to the understanding of its later and fuller development. It underscores the deliberateness of the corruption, the people's mistaken confidence in their own position which proves to be the ground for their final destruction. Long before divine judgment is executed, the people are damned out of their own mouths.

## *Sustaining Involvement: The Use of Metaphor*

I have shown how in the first verse of his book, Ezekiel establishes a cooperative relationship with those whom he addresses by paying them the compliment of familiarity. Moreover, this initial strategy affects his style throughout. Having set a high level of audience alertness, he is able to develop subtle effects which call for discernment and creative interpretation. In fact, he is required to do so. Readers need to exercise the responsibility conferred upon them by the author if they are not to feel let down and therefore less interested in the text and the viewpoint it promotes. It is likely that this need sheds light on one of Ezekiel's most distinctive characteristics, his elaborate use of metaphors. While it may be the case that Ezekiel's taste ran to the baroque (as is frequently claimed in reference to this feature of his style), what can be demonstrated more satisfactorily than his aethetic preference is the practical result of this choice.

The complexity of Ezekiel's use of metaphor remains one of the chief critical issues of the book. Such 'problems' as the frequency with which he combines features from different tradition strands, switches from one image to another, or permits the penetration of the metaphor by undisguised references to historical reality are generally treated in terms of the book's diachronic development. A functional approach, however, while not denying that the text was augmented and changed by editorial hands (including Ezekiel's own), treats the metaphorical discourse as a means by which Ezekiel engages those whom he addresses in a collaborative effort and further shows how the extent and complexity—revealed precisely in these 'problematic' features—of that discourse serve to deepen their relationship.

I have already noted the way in which Ezekiel calls forth and develops figures from earlier prophetic and poetic texts.[32] In elaborating or reifying (in the 'three-dimensional' figures of the sign-actions) these inherited images, the prophet powerfully asserts his identification with the tradition, even as he challenges its current interpretation. This aspect of metaphorical speech—that new figures enter into a literary tradition or a field of established associations which provides the context for their definition—has not received sufficient attention in recent biblical scholarship. On the contrary, biblical hermeneutics has received the strong impress of various tensive theories of metaphor, which tend to emphasize the unexpected, even logically incoherent quality of the associations introduced by this kind of discourse. Ricoeur contrasts his theory of metaphorical tension with the view of classical rhetoric, that metaphorical speech involves simple substitution of ornamental statements for plain ones. Substitution theory thus sees the value of metaphor as purely aesthetic and identifies no communicative function which it is peculiarly qualified to perform. But for Ricoeur, the importance of metaphor resides precisely in the fact that it is a 'semantic impertinence', an innovative form of expression 'which has no status in established language and which exists only in the attribution of unusual predicates'.[33]

The notion that metaphor often involves unprecedented linguistic maneuvers is illuminating, but with respect to biblical texts, undue emphasis on this aspect may disguise another, at least equally important facet. For much of the power of biblical imagery, and especially Ezekiel's, derives from its relation to earlier language. Ezekiel is not content to overthrow the familiar, as any clever *parvenu* could do. More often, his strategy is to work with patterns already established in texts or in popular usage, many of them metaphorical (as, for instance, with the pot image treated above). He shows his genius and his mastery of the tradition by appropriating its symbols, then complicating and deepening them.[34] Even more significantly, he shows his commonality with those to whom the symbols are meaningful and leads them in turn into a more reflective engagement with the tradition.

A second way in which Ezekiel uses familiarity to his advantage is the repetition and variation of his own images. Thus a figure such as the vine is enriched, not only through reverberations with other texts,[35] but also by the echoes set up within Ezekiel's own prophecy. One usage serves to comment upon another. The vine is seen first in its inherent worthlessness (15.3-5), then in wayward growth (17.7-8[36]), and finally in lofty height (19.11). That the height is itself open to condemnation is not evident from 19.10-14; on the basis of this passage alone, it might be inferred that the vine's conspicuousness made it an easy and attractive target for the east wind, but not that it was on that account a deserving one. But the allusion to wrath (19.12) indicates that there was indeed provocation, and a knowledge of Ezekiel's iconography and themes suggests its nature. On the basis of the previous passages in Ezekiel (as well as Jer. 2.21; Hos. 10.1; cf. Isa. 5.1-7; Hos. 9.16), the integrity of the plant, even while it appears to be flourishing, is suspect. Moreover, the foreign oracles repeatedly single out self-elevation (גבה לב, 28.2, 5; cf. 27.3; 29.3) as the root sin of the prosperous. The distortion whereby the prominence which should be a cause of gratitude to the divine benefactor becomes rather a source of pride is central to another plant figure, that of the cedar in ch. 31, which parallels this passage in its vocabulary: בין עבתים ('among the clouds'[37]) and גבה קומה ('height [was] exalted'), 31.3, 5, 10; cf. 19.11; מים רבים ('abundant waters'), 31.5; cf. 19.10. The same charge of godless pride leveled against Assyria[38] (and, by extension, Egypt) can be read back from that figure and directed against Israel.

Seen against the background of the figure's earlier use, aspects of this description emerge more distinctly. In contrast to ch. 15, which declared the vine to be unfit even for kitchen pegs, here it appears that the vine did once have considerable worth: it was meant for ruler's scepters (19.11). But the dignity for which it was intended only sharpens the contrast with the condition to which it has been reduced by a series of destructive operations: violent uprooting, desiccating blasts of the East Wind, transplanting to arid soil, (spontaneous?) combustion. The sources of destruction are drawn from previous appearances of the figure: the fire from ch. 15, uprooting and the East Wind from ch. 17. Now triply condemned, the vine is killed and overkilled; that surplus of devastation climaxes and concludes Ezekiel's use of the image.

Ezekiel's fond replaying of themes gives his readers an opportunity to develop their own mastery of his symbol system. Thus they become able to fill in the gaps in the text, and their attention is rewarded with an enhanced appreciation of its fine effects and cumulative impact. But still that does not make interpretation a certain enterprise. As will be shown below, the text continues to offer ambiguity, multiplicity of meaning, the possibility for development in unexpected directions; and a mastery of the rules only gives the reader a better understanding of what a difficult game this prophet has set.

## Metaphor and Interpretation: Chapter 17

Among the most interesting of Ezekiel's uses of metaphor is the one found in ch. 17, when the prophet is commanded to 'spin a riddle and propound a paradigm' (חוד חידה ומשל משל, 17.2) to the house of Israel. The introductory terms are arresting, first as another indication of Ezekiel's pronounced *Formbewußtsein*,[39] but more importantly for what they suggest about the challenge with which he presents his audience.[40] Here Ezekiel uses the term משל to designate an extended figure (cf. 24.3). Like the more common biblical usage, denoting a brief traditional saying, this kind of משל offers insight into a problematic situation by proposing a likeness, and it, too, requires decoding of culturally informed images. But the fact that this passage is designated also as a חידה ('riddle') indicates that the process of decoding is in this case likely to be particularly complex. Whereas the manifest intention of the משל is to resolve a difficulty and reduce the tension of everyday life (although, as has been seen, it does not always do so in a straightforward manner), the חידה quite deliberately exploits the ambiguous character of reality, usually posing a question which either embodies a seemingly irresolvable contradiction or misleadingly points in one, readily discernible direction, while the correct answer lies in quite another.[41]

Critical commentators have generally assumed that Ezekiel is here reworking a popular fable. Yet even while subscribing to this view, Zimmerli admits that this conception of the figure is far removed from a popular fable, combining as it does features of plant and animal fables in strongly allegorized form: 'If, in the sphere of Wisdom, the fable could at first communicate timeless truth, in Ezek. 17 it has already full entered into the service of the prophetic preaching of history'.[42] In fact, it is altogether impossible to retrieve from this fable, shaped wholly in accordance with the historical circumstances of sixth-century Israel, the pieces of some 'original' representation of universal human experience.

The historical dimension of the fable is made explicit by the interpretative section (vv. 12b-21) attached to it. Predictably, the unity of the two has been variously challenged in recent years. However, the majority of scholars has always granted the existence of an interpretation section within the original scope of the passage and posited various suggestions for how it might have been reworked and expanded.[43] The studies of Lang and Greenberg have been especially helpful in showing beyond reasonable doubt that the figurative and non-figurative forms of discourse belong together and serve a single rhetorical purpose.[44]

I have examined a variety of devices used by the prophet in order to develop a partnership with his audience. The way in which this passage is framed suggests that the combination of allegory and interpretation is such a device. Here as elsewhere (cf. 12.22; 15.2-3; 18.2, 25, 29; 31.2; 38.17, etc.) Ezekiel poses rhetorical questions inviting the participation of his hearers. In this instance, he not only engages them in interpreting the figure (17.12) but also urges their collaborative judgment on its application to the historical situation (17.15). The question which is crucial for our own interpretation of this text and for a proper understanding of the nature of Ezekiel's role is this: what are the consequences of the engagement which he seeks to elicit? What view of reality is promoted here by this discourse which is throughout informed by, although not strictly confined to, the terms of the allegory?

Lang's work is especially important here, because he is the only contemporary scholar to have given serious consideration to the social role of this prophet. Interpretation of the present chapter is in fact central to his argument that Ezekiel's function is essentially a political one: to foment opposition among the exiles to the anti-Babylonian policies of Zedekiah and those in Jerusalem who were agitating for rebellion. For Lang, the rhetorical power of the passage resides primarily in the questions, which 'summon the hearer to action upon the argument and to a political position'.[45] He supports this view by locating the terms of the figure within the political rhetoric of Israel and Asia. While denying the existence of a *Vorlage* as such, he suggests that such traditional motifs as eagle, cedar, vinestock, and East Wind serve as the building blocks from which Ezekiel constructs a verbal caricature of an icon associated with the Mesopotamian kings, depicting two winged and often birdheaded creatures tending the plant which stands between them.

However, the images which Ezekiel has chosen are more profoundly ambiguous than Lang allows.[46] To say that they belong to the political rhetoric of Israel is an oversimplification. If these motifs are combined in such a way as to mimic the images propagated by Mesopotamian kings, it must not be overlooked that they are also deeply rooted in Israelite iconography; and the literature which has been preserved for us indicates that whatever impact they may have had on the political situation was due to the powerful echoes which they brought to bear upon it from Israel's religious tradition.

It has already been noted that the vine is in the prophetic literature and in the psalms a familiar figure for Israel. On the other hand, the figure of the eagle characterizes YHWH as Israel's rescuer and protector (Exod. 19.4; Deut. 32.11). Lang is correct that the latter image is used repeatedly in connection with Israel's enemies, but the contexts of its appearance resist any ready characterization of the eagle as a political or military symbol. Although there are instances in which foreign armies are specifically compared with the eagle on the point of swiftness (Hab. 1.8; Lam. 4.19), it is striking how frequently there is ambiguity in the interpretation of the figure. In Jer. 48.40 and 49.22, the eagle is compared with an unidentified masculine subject, which may be reasonably inferred to be the Babylonian army. Yet the indefiniteness does not exclude the possibility that the divine oracle speaks here—at least in a secondary sense—of God's own vengeance against Moab and Edom. Even in Deut. 28.49, where the reference is clearly to a foreign army, the emphasis of the passage lies on YHWH's summoning a force to effect the divine curses (28.15) through military activity. With respect to the present passage, the very problematic use of the eagle figure in Hos. 8.1 is especially interesting. It is far from clear, despite Lang,[47] that this 'eagle over the house of YHWH' is a reference to the Assyrians or to any human enemy. If the MT preserves an original reading,[48] then the eagle is already here, as in Ezekiel, conjoined with the notion of transgression of God's covenant, although the connection betwen the two remains unclear.

Moreover, within Ezekiel's fable there is also cause for ambivalent identification of the eagle. One cannot help but hear in the eagle's transport of the sprig to ארץ כנען (17.4)[49] at least a faint echo of the Exodus journey (cf. Exod. 19.4; Deut. 32.11). It is doubtful also whether the extravagant descriptions of the eagle's soliticitude for the vine are really meant to characterize Nebuchadnezzar's attitude toward vassal Israel. Even if one grants that the prophet idealizes the intentions of the Babylonians in order to stress the enormous folly of Zedekiah's defection, it is still tempting, if not unavoidable, to see behind the benevolent eagle YHWH's continuing care for Israel.[50]

A similar effect is created by Ezekiel's introduction of the East Wind. This, too, is associated within the Exodus tradition with God's activity on Israel's behalf (Exod. 10.13; 14.21). In the prophetic literature, the East Wind appears as a figure of destruction aimed at Israel, but again it is unsatisfactory to call it, with Lang, simply an image for the attack of a superior army.[51] In all the instances which Lang himself cites (Hos. 13.15; Isa. 27.8; Jer. 18.17), the real source of terror is the storm force of YHWH, and only in a derivative sense the Assyrians or neo-Babylonians, through whom it is currently manifest.

The ambiguity which Ezekiel cultivates in the fable is reinforced rather than resolved by the interpretative section which follows. This is accomplished chiefly by the way in which the prophet manipulates the language of covenant, moving from what appear to be purely political considerations of a vassal pledge and its violation to God's charge that Zedekiah broke '*my* covenant'—and it is that act of contempt which shall finally be requited on his head. Zimmerli finds no difficulty in reading both references at a single level: 'Behind this there stands a form of covenant according to which the partner taken into covenant by a superior affirmed his loyalty by appealing to his own gods.'[52] This is apparently how the Chronicler read the text (2 Chron. 36.13), but Greenberg challenges the historical basis for this solution: 'Now, that Nebuchadnezzar (or any neo-Babylonian king) imposed on his vassals an oath of allegiance by their own gods is otherwise unknown'.[53]

Whether or not there was a single oath which might be called both Nebuchadnezzar's and YHWH's, the language of this passage causes us to view Zedekiah's acts of violation from a shifting perspective. The kaleidoscope turns as Ezekiel works changes on the recurrent phrase, הפר ברית ... בזה אלה ('despise oath ... break covenant'). In the first of its three appearances (17.16), the nouns are qualified—'*his* oath. . . *his* covenant'—so as to refer clearly to Nebuchadnezzar. No pronominal suffixes appear in the second instance of the phrase (v. 18). Although the context favors the assumption that the referent is still the Babylonian king, it is noteworthy that precisely this unqualified form of the phrase is used in 16.59, where it serves as a summary description of Israel's apostasy. The muting of the political reference in 17.18 and the echo with the distinctly theological sense of the earlier passage makes the transition less abrupt when, in the third occurrence of the phrase (v. 19), the outrage is seen to have been perpetrated against YHWH.

It is a mistake to separate political from theological elements, human from divine planes in any absolute way. The text should not be read as a strict allegory, in which each element has a single correct interpretation. The historical richness of the images resists such reductionism, as does Ezekiel's pleonastic style.[54] Moreover, in view of the theme of God's honor which is the hallmark, even the obsession of this prophet, it seems perverse to subordinate the genuinely theological concern to the political one. Ezekiel creates a literary structure which leads to a much more complex perception of the interaction between the two spheres of activity and meaning. As has been seen, the images of the fable belong at least as much to theology as to politics, and if the interpretation seems at first to direct us to the latter, we are not long allowed to retain that single focus. The decoding of the figure in terms of the vassal relationship between Nebuchadnezzar and Zedekiah itself becomes a kind of figure illustrating the relationship between Israel and YHWH.[55] Seen through Ezekiel's eyes, the world is inescapably theocentric; articulated through divine speech, the interpretation of experience must finally be rendered in theological terms.

However, there is a tension between the allegory and the

interpretation, one troublesome enough to cast doubt upon a synchronic reading of the chapter in its final form. The problem lies, not in any presumed incompatibility between figurative and literal language,[56] but rather at the level of content. The historical accuracy of the allusion to Pharaoh's failure to relieve besieged Jerusalem (17.17) makes it suspect as a part of the original pre-fall prophecy. That there is a linguistic relationship with 17.9 is obvious, but their logical reconciliation is difficult. Verse 9 anticipates (wrongly, as it turned out), that the great eagle will be able to uproot the vine of Judah easily, 'not with a mighty arm or a great multitude' ( ולא־בזרע גדולה ובעם־רב). Verse 17 applies a similar phrase to a different world power, producing a correct (ostensible) prediction: 'And not with a mighty force or a great assembly (ולא בחיל גדול ובקהל רב) will Pharaoh deal with him (i.e., Nebuchadnezzar) in war.' Further, it directly contradicts v. 9 in acknowledging how elaborate is the Babylonian siege effort required to topple Jerusalem.

Greenberg and Lang maintain the fundamental synchronicity of the two verses by adopting a solution earlier put forward by Kraetzschmar: פרעה ('Pharaoh', v. 17) is a gloss. Originally, then, v. 17 stood in agreement with v. 9, but its form was open to manipulation of meaning with relatively little verbal change. The vague verbal phrase יעשה אותו, specifying neither subject nor object, can apply equally to Nebuchadnezzar's siege of Jerusalem or to Hophra's weakly attempted opposition to Nebuchadnezzar.[57] However, this nod to a gloss, while syntactically feasible, does not really produce a satisfactory reading of the verse. The fairly full description of the formidable siegeworks in v. 17b is more appropriate to the present usage, where it contrasts sadly with Pharaoh's puny relief force, than to the posited original sense of the passage (i.e., a prediction that Nebuchadnezzar would expend no great effort to bring down Jerusalem).[58]

Indeed, the appeal to a glossator (which, Greenberg concedes, may be the prophet himself) betrays the weakness of the strict synchronic position. Although admitting the thin end of the wedge of diachronic development, it fails to reckon adequately with the significance of that development for our understanding of the text. While upholding the basic unity of fable and interpretation, I wish to press the issue of diachronic development further than Greenberg and Lang allow, for it is precisely by pushing in this direction that the hermeneutical richness of the text is revealed. Incorporation of the interpretation as an essential element of the prophetic word is itself a hermeneutical move of great significance. A comparison of the present passage with Isaiah's song of the vineyeard (5.1-7) is instructive. In both cases, the prophet's hearers are directly summoned to render judgment on a fictional situation presented in figurative terms. In both cases, also, the prophet offers some guidance for application of the figurative discourse (and the judgment accorded it) to the audience's own circumstances. But the two prophets differ in the degree to which they commit themselves to historical contingency. The earlier prophet represents the failed relationship between God and Judah and the punishment which God will exact. Yet within the scope of the parable, it never becomes clear precisely what form the vengeance will take or when it will occur. Removal of protecting hedge and wall suggests enemy invasion; the prohibition of rain, drought. The eventuality of both forms of disaster was a fairly safe bet in ancient Israel; the odds were that, sooner rather than later, the prophecy would be proved correct.

In formulating his fable, Ezekiel took the risk of drastically lowering the level of abstraction. The first indication of this occurs within the fable itself, where the reality of warfare is allowed to penetrate the façade of the non-human world (ולא־בזרע גדולה ובעם־רב, 'not with a mighty arm or a great multitude', v. 9). But the extended interpretation section makes it clear that Ezekiel has gone an important step beyond Isaiah in delineating the execution of Israel's fate at God's hands in concrete political terms. Moreover, if the basic premise of this study is correct, he took the greater risk of committing himself to that specific vision *in writing*. And it was that move which both required and facilitated his engagement with hermeneutics to a degree unprecedented in prophecy.

With respect to the text's diachronic development, the interesting thing about the interpretation section in ch. 17 is not that it translates the metaphorical terms of the fable into realistic language; as we have seen, these may well belong to a single level of composition. Rather, it is the fact that, on this one point concerning the fall of the city, the interpretation shows itself to be bound by the language of the fable, while yet forced to contradict its plain meaning. Circumstances proved v. 9 to be wrong; Jerusalem yielded only to a long siege and great military effort. As with the mistaken prophecy about Tyre, Ezekiel was obliged to correct his own earlier statement.[59] But this time, rather than replacing the erroneous oracle with a new and admittedly later one, he employed a more oblique hermeneutical strategy. By creating a near-echo of v. 9 in the opening phrase of v. 17, the prophet established a linkage which might at first glance appear to be affirming. Moreover, while neither possible sense of v. 17's יעשה אותו (which must, in this context, mean either 'deal with' Nebuchadnezzar as an enemy or Zedekiah as an ally) accords with v. 9's clear phrase, למשאות אותה משרשיה ('to pull it up from its roots'), its very vagueness avoids a direct conflict. The effect is to draw the earlier, mistaken prophecy into the sphere of the later interpretation, where its content receives a subtle reinterpretation. That the strategy was as least partially successful is shown by the way in which Rashi (as also Joseph Kara and David Kimḥi) reads the content from v. 17 back into v. 9: '"Not with a mighty arm or a great multitude" will the second eagle come to their aid... to confront those who pull it up and transport it from its roots.'

In my opinion, a fairly strong case can be made for viewing vv. 16-18 altogether as a later portion of the interpretation.[60] However, the hermeneutical point is really no different than if only a single word was inserted. By attaching a non-figurative interpretation to his fable, Ezekiel anchors it firmly in historical reality. If this technique brings his oracle directly into the mainstream of Israel's political and theological discourse, it also makes all the more evident the contingency and possible error which are inescapable elements of living prophecy. Of course, the risk of exposure is greatly magnified by inscription of the prophetic word. In view of the perpetual tension between the fixed text and the context of interpretation, which changed significantly even within the period of the prophet's own activity, this dimension must not be dissolved. The diachronic development of the text enables its adaptation to new historical circumstances. It is therefore an essential element of the prophecy's vitality and openness to reality. It follows, then, that these additions to the text, while secondary in a chronological sense, belong to its basic fabric (a connection which the word 'gloss' overlooks). Indeed, they grow out of the hermeneutical structure which Ezekiel built into his composition from the beginning, through both the interpretation section proper and the inclusion of a realistic reference within the fable (v. 9). With these additions, the text extends its compass and thus acquires a new (but not distorted) literary shape and a rhetorical purpose more adequate to its status as a permanent record.

In addition to explicating what precedes it, the present form of the interpretation section also serves to draw the fable into interaction with other prophetic texts. This is most evident from v. 20, which introduces the new figure of the hunting net and uses terminology closely parallel to that of the lion hunt in ch. 19: פרש עליו רשת 'spread a net over him', נתפש 'captured', במצוה 'in [a] snare', הביא בבלה /אל־מלך בבל 'bring to Babylon/to the king of Babylon' (cf. 19.8-9).[61] Thus the portrayal of Zedekiah is brought into the sphere of that other allegory which, precisely because it lacks historical specificity, functions as a comprehensive judgment on the monarchy. While attempts have, of course, been made to identify the two lion cubs and their mother with particular figures, no solution is entirely satisfactory.[62] Here, stereotypic concepts seem to have prevailed over particular representation: Israel's kings are ravaging lions who despoil their own land, and their mete punishment is expulsion from it. It is likely that the pattern of geographically balanced exiles which appears in the allegory is neither fortuitous nor historically determined but rather shows the influence of earlier prophecy, viz., Hosea's depiction of parallel wanderings or deportations of YHWH's people, to West and to East (Hos. 7.11; 9.3; cf. 11.11; 12.2). The effect of drawing together the two allegories is that both are strengthened. Zedekiah's well-known machinations give substance to the categorical charge against the royal house; and in turn, the fate which Ezekiel declares for him is anticipated and confirmed by echoes of prophecy whose authority is already long established.

Another significant change occurs with the departure from the imagery of the fable: when YHWH emerges in 17.20 as the self-declared hunter and judge of Israel's king, the perspective returns to the unambiguously theocentric one characteristic of the book. The gradual shift in orientation from a political to a theological frame of reference, adumbrated in the changing use of covenant language (vv. 15-19), is completed with this verse.

This theocentric perspective is retained when Ezekiel once again takes up the eagle image in vv. 22-24. The identification of the great eagle with God, which, as I have suggested, is never quite lost as a possibility hovering in the background of the fable, here comes strongly (note the emphatic אני in v. 22) to the fore in a promise of restoration. The common dating of these verses after the fall is probable,[63] although they serve a central function within the final form of the passage. As the interpretation section brings the world of the fable into ongoing dialogue with the world of historical contingency, so the restoration promise opens it up to the future. The notion that the chapter achieved this shape only over the course of time does nothing to diminish its integrity. Rather, it shows how the richness of the prophet's original conception gradually yielded a literary product of great complexity. If the diachronic development was indeed something like what I have sketched, then Ezekiel's own interpretive process moved from the political sphere (vv. 12-15) to the theological (v. 19), and then later to a further specification of political events (vv. 16-18) and an extension of the theological perspective into an eschatalogical vision (vv. 22-24). The reader faces the challenge of perceiving the interrelationship and interpenetration of these different levels of reality. The multifaceted text that sets this task is rightly called both משל and חירה.

## Chapter 5

## VISION IN HISTORY

This is the use of memory:
For liberation—not less of love but expanding
Of love beyond desire, and so liberation
From the future as well as the past. Thus, love of a country
Begins as attachment to our own field of action
And comes to find that action of little importance
Though never indifferent. History may be servitude,
History may be freedom. See, now they vanish,
The faces and places, with the self which, as it could, loved them,
To become renewed, transfigured, in another pattern.

(T.S. Eliot, *Little Gidding*)

From a form-critical perspective, one of the most exceptional features of Ezekiel's prophecy is the prominence of extended narrative accounts of various kinds: historical (ch. 20), allegorical (chs. 16; 23), visionary (chs. 1; 8-11; 40-48). Gunkel viewed his frequent use of a new genre, *Geschichteserzählung*, as a natural development of the political situation and the prophet's role within it: 'What is more natural for a politician, than to recall the past in order to create from it a lesson for the present?'[1] Thus, he contends, Israel's last prophets inculcate (*einschärfen*) their abstract thoughts, and prophecy moves toward historical philosophy (*Geschichtesphilosophie*).

While Gunkel is concerned with the formal aspect of the narratives, Kaufmann takes a different approach. For him, it is their content which is noteworthy and also problematic. The visions and the histories are likewise 'products of an exuberant imagination',[2] worthless as representations of Israelite religious practice. Kaufmann is surely right to see Ezekiel's histories as imaginative creations, and not only because of their extravagant metaphorical garb. No one ever recounted Israel's past as Ezekiel does; he presents the most radical revisioning of the tradition, going back to the beginning of the nation's history, and showing it to be a consistent record of rebellion and apostasy. Thus he provides the depth dimension to his protrayal of the doomed nation. Israel's very pedigree is pagan (16.3); the period in Egypt was one of willful harlotry (23.3) and idol-worship (20.8); there was no honeymoon in the wilderness (cf. Jer. 2.1; Hos. 2.17), but only blatant unfaithfulness. S.R. Driver comments regarding Ezekiel's freedom with the past that 'he has transferred to it unconsciously the associations of the present'.[3] Greenberg responds: 'Ezekiel was equally unjust to the present, unconsciously transferring to *it* the associations of Manasseh's age'.[4]

Yet neither the form-critical approach nor the historical one renders a satisfactory account of Ezekiel's narratives. Certainly, if the prophet intended to produce either historical philosophy or historiography, then the attempt must be reckoned a failure. On the one hand, both the histories and the visions are in fact very different from anything which might be termed *Geschichtesphilosophie*. In so far as they are effective, it is precisely because they are not abstract, but rather shockingly concrete renderings of the inexorable progression from sin to judgment. It is not a philosophical discourse but a story which Ezekiel is telling, and he tells it fully and graphically, drawing his images with painstaking care in the documentation of abomination and abandonment, then carrying those same images forward as he delineates the future hope. On the other hand, the notion of 'unconscious transference' would certainly discredit Ezekiel as an accurate reporter of events, if that were the purpose of his writing. But one must doubt the validity of a method which imposes modern standards for veridical history on Ezekiel and then criticizes his failure to measure up to them. I would prefer to assume that this skillful manipulator of words accomplished what he set out to do and that he chose the unusual (for a prophet) vehicle of narrative speech as the means best suited to further that end. It is the purpose of this chapter to show that what he achieves is a deliberate and thorough reconceptualization of Israel's past and present, and that conveying this reconceptualization is a crucial element of Ezekiel's prophetic enterprise, for it is only by this means that the future can be claimed.

## The Function of Narrative

A pragmatic approach to the question of Ezekiel's use of narrative should be formulated along the following lines: to what sort of communicative task is narrative discourse particularly suited, and how does Ezekiel exploit its potential in the service of prophecy? The function of narrative is an aspect of practical poetics which has received wide attention in recent years; work in this area may contribute to an appreciation of Ezekiel's unprecedented use of the form.

Narrative may be simply defined as 'a sequenced representation of incidents, produced by someone and for someone'.[5] The most important thing which follows from this definition is that narratives are not direct reproductions of reality; they are works of art, created by the human mind and intended for an audience. They are, in other words, a form of social interaction. This conception implies the inadequacy of analyses which treat narratives solely in terms of either their formal properties or their relation to the historical situation they purport to represent without regard for the situation of telling.

In order to evaluate the success of a given narrative as a form of social interaction, it is important to ascertain what it is that narratives are meant to achieve. Pratt's perceptive observation concerning 'natural' (non-literary) narratives might well be applied more generally:[6]

> ... natural narratives invariably deal with states of affairs that are held to be unusual and problematic, in need of experiential and evaluative resolution.... One of the most important ways we have of dealing with the unexpected, uncertain, unintelligible aspects of our lives is to share and interpret them collectively. Carrying out this recreative, interpretive process is one of the most important uses we make of language.[7]

Narratives are designed to help us live in the world, not primarily to convey new information about it. Story-telling is an inefficient means of imparting facts, but it may sometimes be the only way we are brought to reckon with, in Dr. Johnson's phrase, 'truths too important to be new'. Narrative production as a component of various activities—dreaming, play, moral teaching, religious observance, novel or history writing—is essential to the multiform task of conceiving and manipulating hypothetical worlds or conditions, and mediating the relations between them and our present situations, as well as the values that inform both.

The relation between narrative and historical reality is therefore a complex one. Narratives are designed to treat concrete problems which arise in specific historical conditions, and narrative solutions reflect the social conventions, relations, and communicative intentions obtaining among particular individuals and groups. All stories, whether they refer to real or to imaginary events, have an historical dimension, for they reflect the fact that as human beings we are enmeshed in temporality and contingency. Yet it is also true that we tell them, if not actually to escape the confines of the immediate situation, then to gain a little distance from them, so that we may perceive more clearly the patterns and limitations of our condition. And we tell our stories to others because we imagine (and, happily, we are often correct) that they have a significance which extends beyond our own personal experience. We narrate, then, in order to enlarge our sense of possibility and sphere of active concern. We memorialize the past or evoke the imaginary in such a way as to create a dialectic between the familiar and the forgotten or alien. History, no less than fiction, 'explores the field of "imaginative" variations which surround the present and the real we take for granted in everyday life'.[8]

The selection of material is a further aspect of the way narrative is adapted to the situation of telling. Selection is the basic skill of narrative art, for 'incidents' are not read off directly from reality. They are a function of the narrator's perceptions and communicative intentions: moments drawn from the continuum of actual or fictional life, imaginatively refined into discrete elements, combined into a pattern ('the plot') which can be grasped as a whole. And if narrative is to be understood as a form of social interaction, then the question to be asked is what motivates this process of selection and recombination. Ricoeur treats this question perceptively, drawing upon W.B. Gallie's[9] notion that a plot initiates a 'teleologically guided' movement:

> ... the 'conclusion' of the story is the pole of attraction of the whole process. But a narrative conclusion can be neither deduced nor predicted. There is no story unless our attention is held in suspense by a thousand contingencies. Hence we must follow the

story to its conclusion. So rather than being *predictable*, a conclusion must be *acceptable*.[10]

The significance of this teleological orientation of narrative emerges more fully when considered in conjunction with Pratt's observations about the way we tell stories in order to examine the unintelligible aspects of our lives and reach some shared interpretation or resolution. Narrated events are selected and ordered to create an impression of continuity and meaning in place of what seemed to be randomness, rupture, chaos. This is something quite different from the common view that plot relations are designed to display causality. For both the problems and the solutions associated with narrative belong more to the order of interpretation than of rule-governed logic. If the aim of a plot were to show how one event determines another, then it could be of little interest or help to those caught in problematic situations, in whom the successful demonstration of inevitability generates only passivity or despair. But narrative is directed toward eliciting emotional and cognitive involvement in the discovery that a given sequence of occurrences, however difficult, has a coherence and an outcome which may be deemed 'acceptable after all'. Rather than speaking of narrative as demonstrating causality, it may be more satisfactory to say that it discloses the intelligibility of our experience and thus confers upon it a kind of validation. When the narrative has a transcendent perspective, it is not too much to say that it seeks to demonstrate justice.

## The Use of Memory

The teleological orientation and the demonstrative function of narrative are important in understanding Ezekiel's use of the genre as a distinctive feature of his prophecy. Previous prophets issued threats and warnings in hope of bringing Israel to a halt on the edge of the precipice. But Ezekiel begins with the assumption of disaster; the collapse of the holy city and the throne of David is the consistent focal point for the first part of the book (chs. 1-24), where the histories appear. He, too, is concerned with Israel's survival, but that issue is now bound inextricably with the problem of theodicy. Israel's future as YHWH's people depends upon their ability to reconcile this thing which was never supposed to happen with what they know—or should have known—of their God (14.23). So his prophecy is more than a warning; it is designed to serve an explanatory function, to explain a state of affairs which is, in terms of the regnant theological system, quite literally unthinkable. Against the sacred tradition of an inviolate Zion, Ezekiel must show that God's judgment on Judah and Jerusalem is fully warranted as the grim consequence of Israel's conduct. Greenberg wrongly asserts that the prophet's view of Israel's history is a 'perspectiveless, organic whole'.[11] It is, indeed, the very opposite: a highly artificial synthesis of Israel's experience, viewed from what seemed to be its end, the collapse which only on the basis of that history can be judged acceptable after all.

The character of Ezekiel's histories, then, must be understood in relation to the situation of telling. And it would seem to be precisely by virtue of their artificiality, i.e., the high degree of schematization which inevitably distances them from the diffuseness and ambiguity of real life, that these histories were effective. Greenberg acknowledges this with respect to the people's willingness to accept the representation of Israel's history as one of undifferentiated sin, even in contradiction of available evidence. His comments upon Ezekiel's achievement are congruent with the foregoing discussion regarding the function of narrative:

> Susceptibility to a doctrine is a function of its need. In a catastrophe, the need for finding intelligibility is existential: unless one can find some pattern in events, disintegration and collapse must ensue. . . . In this crisis, the systematizer Ezekiel provided a remedy. . . . Ezekiel's recasting of the past was the only way to bring history under the yoke of intelligibility, to show that it followed rules.[12]

I would doubt only the suggestion that Ezekiel is concerned to show that history follows rules. There is considerable disparity between the way he uses case law (ch. 18) to set forth the predictable execution of divine retribution and, on the other hand, the pattern evidenced by the historical survey, where Ezekiel is at pains to assert that time and again the rules were broken by God in order to spare Israel (20.9, 14, 17, 22), though to no avail. It is not with the aim of establishing the objective order of reality as evidenced in historical phenomena (*Geschichtesphilosophie*) that the prophet creates his narratives. Rather he is concerned with reorganizing Israel's view of its past from the standpoint of the present crisis.[13] He seeks to give Israel a new sense of history as a basis for future faith.

Nowhere is the reorienting force of this retrospectivity more evident than in ch. 20. The major critical problem of this section is determining its original scope: specifically, the relation of the future prospect to the historical summary. Zimmerli sees the summary alone as primary and derives its basic outline (in vv. 5-26) from the historical credo identified by von Rad as the core of Israelite tradition. Verses 32-44 are considered an addition, a post-fall promise of salvation which takes the form of a disputation saying. While it is certainly plausible that the passage underwent diachronic development, the attempt to make such a sharp division in its present form on the basis of chronology and sense seems misguided on several counts.

First, the credo analogy fits awkwardly even within Zimmerli's analysis of the first part of the chapter. He takes vv. 27-29 to be the work of a glossator, who 'has overlooked the close connection of the original oracle to the outline of the credo and has attempted to add briefly a reference to Israel's history in the land, which is missing in the credo and which is also a history of sin'.[14] The logic of this argument is elusive, since all the basic credo formulations found by von Rad (Deut. 6.20-24; 26.5-9; Josh. 24.2-13) presuppose settlement. Moreover, if these verses are omitted, there is no condemnation of Israel's cultic practice in the land of Israel itself, which is clearly of paramount significance to Ezekiel and would provide the chief point of contrast between Israel's conduct as represented in this passage and that prescribed in the instructions for the harvest sacrifice in the archetypal credo of Deuteronomy 26.

Further, Zimmerli's reading requires that vv. 30-31 be seen as the original conclusion to the piece, although they include no formula to indicate closure. Never, in any of its sixteen occurrences in the book, does the oath formula (חי אני 'by my life') perform such a function. Rather it makes an asseveration of which the amplification follows (16.48; 18.3; 20.3; 33.11), frequently confirming a pronouncement of judgment (14.16, 18, 20; 17.16) or marking a transition from reproach to judgment (5.11; 17.19; 33.27; 35.6, 11). Perhaps the closest usage to this one (v. 31) is that in 34.8, where it sums up a previous accusation against the negligent shepherds, gathering momentum for the proclamation (as one would think) of judgment—although what follows is instead a proclamation of salvation concerning the flock itself.

The proclamation which follows the summation in ch. 20 (with a

repetition of the oath formula in v. 33) is not, at least in any
straightforward sense, a promise of salvation. This is clear from a
comparison with the related passage, 36.16-38, delineating the divine
response-in-action (עוד זאת אדרש לבית-ישראל לעשות להם 'Moreover,
thus will I respond to the house of Israel and act on their behalf',
v. 37), which is still withheld from Israel at the time of the present
inquiry (cf. 20.3, 31). Chapters 20 and 36 look to the same events, the
gathering of the exiles for purgation and their return to their own
land, but from widely disparate perspectives. The difference is
between a minatory tone and a soothing one, between, on the one
hand, emphasizing the harsh excision of 'the rebels and the sinners'
(20.38)—and one must assume, on the basis of Ezekiel's frequent
characterization of Israel as בית מרי ('a rebellious house'), that he
expected this to be the majority—and, on the other, looking to a
condition of wholeness which surpasses that preceding affliction
when a people infused with a new heart and a new spirit (36.26) will
dwell on a land lush as Eden (36.35). If 20.32-44 shows the way into
the future, it nonetheless stands as a threat and a warning of how few
it is to whom the future is open.

But the greatest weakness of Zimmerli's judgment about the late
dating of 20.32-44 is that it rests upon his improbable reading of v. 32
as an expression of resignation after the burning of Jerusalem, to
which the prophet responds with a message of consolation proclaiming
'the great joy that God remains at work, even through the darkest
night of his people'.[15] While the reported saying is itself ambiguous,
its placement in the first part of the book would argue for contrast,
not equation, with clear expressions of despair (33.10; 37.11) cited in
direct connection with the fall. The similarity to 1 Sam. 8.20, a
faithless and ill-fated wish spoken to God's prophet by another
delegation of elders, also supports the view that the statement quoted
is meant to be understood as an optative and therefore as the fullest
expression of Israel's rebellious disposition toward its God. Moreover,
the final phrase, לשרת עץ ואבן ('serving wood and stone')—surely the
prophet's own addition—shows the tone of this verse to be consistent
with that ironic distance from popular sentiment and theology which
characterizes the whole history.

Taken as a statement of desire, v. 32 can be seen to have a
connection with both parts of the speech and thus to serve as a pivot
between the two. It is Israel's aspiration which motivates the prophet

to take a sweeping view of the nation's history, both backward and forward. The purpose of the recitation is oppositional: thus the prophet asserts that being like the nations is not and has never been an option for Israel, for its status is uniquely bound up with YHWH's honor. And that honor will be vindicated. God will again take Israel out from among the nations 'with a strong hand and an outstretched arm', but this time Israel will be the object of the same driving force and furious wrath once vented against the Egyptians (vv. 33-34).

Moreover, the scope of the sweep is determined by Israel's current position in exile. 'The boundaries of the retrospect have been determined by those of the prospect':[16] as it is only by another exodus and wilderness experience that Israel may anticipate return to its land, so those are the features which Ezekiel highlights from the tradition. It is, then, not the case that he follows some predetermined historical outline or credo to produce a parody of the tradition, which is later supplemented with a somewhat haphazard collection of later additions. Rather, retrospect and prospect belong together as complementary dimensions of a new narrative, whose elements have been selected and shaped in accordance with the situation of telling.

But, granted that the history has been schematized according to the requirements of the present situation, nonetheless Ezekiel's sovereignty over the tradition is striking. Nowhere is this so evident as in the hard saying of v. 25:

> And for my part, I gave them laws which were not good and statutes by which they could not live. And I profaned them by their own gifts, in that they delivered over every first issue of the womb, so that I might desolate them, that they might know that I am YHWH.

Various suggestions have been advanced to lessen the shock of this assertion. Torrey offers a syntactical alternative, reading the sentences as interrogatives ('Did I at all give them statutes which were not good. . .?'), to which the implied answer is, of course, 'No'. Yet there is no syntactical indication that these statements are not to be read in the same declarative manner as the rest of the survey (contrast the marked interrogatives in 14.3; 15.4; 17.15; 18.29, etc.). Zimmerli raises the possibility of making a semantic distinction between חוקים and חוקות (cf. v. 11) as, respectively, the harmful and the saving will of God, and of seeing the circumlocution לא טובים ('not good') as a further softening, but the distinction is too nice to carry conviction.[17] Likewise unsatisfactory are historical explanations which would attempt to show that Ezekiel was just reporting the facts; there is no evidence that the demands of Exod. 22.28b and 34.19a were taken categorically at an early period in Israel's history.[18] Carroll's suggestion that the commandments are 'designed as a primitive form of aversion therapy'[19] hardly commends itself. Eichrodt and Greenberg try to show precedent by comparing the passage to the hardening of Pharaoh's heart; similarly, Rashi observes: 'This is the idea of causing sin in order to magnify punishment.' But finding an analogy does not point to an accepted line of interpretation (cf. the directly contrary statements on the law of sacrifice in Jer. 7.31; 19.5; 32.35). Moreover, the theological implications of the analogy are hardly comparable. It is one thing to say that God hardened the heart of the enemy, thereby causing Israel temporary difficulty for the sake of greater vindication, and quite another to claim that there was a fundamental subversion in the law, which is both God's greatest act of self-revelation and also the gift by which Israel comes to know itself as God's own people, and thus literally the source of its life.

The statement resists all attempts at domestication. Its power lies precisely in the fact that it cannot be conformed to human reason. This verse reasserts, indeed, carries to its illogical extreme what is Ezekiel's constant theme: the indisputable authority of God to determine and interpret the course of human history. The prophet declares that this loathsome 'gift', the injunction to child sacrifice, resembles the life-giving statutes and sabbaths (vv. 11-12) in that it also proceeds from God's initiative. He locates this initiative even behind that aspect of Israel's conduct which is most abominable to God and would seem to fall solely in the sphere of pagan influence.[20] So Israel cannot be like the nations, no matter how assiduously it seeks to deny the association with YHWH by departing from anything recognizable as the law of that God. Even Israel's willful self-destruction is, however inexplicably, an outworking of the sovereign will of YHWH.

The divine initiative manifests itself in another way, less jarring but almost as surprising, within this passage. The final section is remarkable in its reversal of the usual sequence of Israel's recognition and repentance of sin, followed by a divine act of restoration, signalling forgiveness:

> And you will know that I am YHWH, when I have brought you to
> the soil of Israel, to the land which I swore to give to your
> ancestors, and there you will recall your ways and all your deeds by
> which you were defiled, and you will loathe yourselves for all the
> evil acts which you performed (vv. 42-43).

Yet such a reversal (expressed also in 16.59-63) is fully consonant
with the theocentric emphasis of the book and represents one of the
most profound biblical insights into the affective logic of reconciliation.
Dante correctly perceived that the condition of radical separation
from God—hell—is better imaged by ice than by flames. Habituation
to sin brings increasing immobilization, so that we become finally
unable to choose another course (cf. Jer. 13.23). Therefore, however
just the punishment of exile may be, that in itself cannot bring Israel
to self-recognition and thus to repentance. Only God's *prior* act of
deliverance from the effects of sin makes it possible for Israel to stand
at some critical distance from its own conduct. Encouraged by the
demonstration of God's undeserved favor, the nation can begin to
make proper use of its memory by entering into an honest assessment
of the past and assuming full responsibility for what it has done.

In two narrative passages, Israel's remembering is mentioned
specifically in connection with the divine recognition formula (16.61-
63; 20.42-44; cf. 23.49), thus underscoring the central point of
Ezekiel's message: that Israel knows itself only *vis à vis* YHWH and
through acknowledgment of the actions by which YHWH is revealed
as its sole and sovereign God. For Israel, remembering the past and
acknowledging YHWH are inseparable elements of a complex
interaction.[21] Israel is brought to recognize YHWH through the same
kind of restorative acts by which it was first constituted as a nation.
These stir Israel's memory and sense of shame at its own deeds, and
the contrast between its deserving and what YHWH has done leads to
a deeper understanding of this God before whom Israel stands for
judgment and blessing.

Similarly, it is in terms of divine initiative, as creating the
conditions for human responsibility, that the notion of the לב בשר
('heart of flesh', 11.19; 36.26) must be understood. The connection is
underscored by the fact that the phrase appears in the passage related
to this one as the continuation of Israel's history from a post-
destruction perspective.[22] The pledge of a new heart in ch. 36
corresponds to the bad laws in ch. 20 as the good gift, making

possible Israel's true life of obedience to YHWH, which replaces the 'anti-gift', whereby the very concept of obedience was rendered inoperative. But it is no more true that the divinely given heart of flesh obviates human responsibility than that the first bestowal removed Israel's culpability. Contrary to Kaufmann, who sees here 'the eschatological vision of the new heart that man is to get at the end of days which will render him incapable of sinning',[23] Ezekiel holds out to the exiles a promise susceptible of realization even in their own time. He envisions, not a new creation which eliminates the element of willful obedience, but rather a radical act of forgiveness which frees Israel from the burden, though not the memory, of the past and renders it capable of hearing, of forming new habits, and of entering into a new relationship with YHWH.[24]

The fact that Ezekiel ends his history with a vision of restoration does not disguise the fact that it remains throughout a narrative of alienation. The genius and also the difficulty of the piece consist in this: it is history told from the perspective of one standing outside the dominant cultural tradition. This is evident from the irony which pervades his historical review and from the particular targets on which he focuses it: the Exodus tradition (ביד חזקה ובזרוע נטויה ובחמה שפוכה 'with a strong hand and with an outstretched arm and with outpoured wrath', vv. 33-34), the giving of the law (v. 25), the cult (vv. 28-29, 32), the covenant (v. 37). Turning one of the sharpest weapons in his arsenal against the fundaments of the tradition, this prophet exercises his fierce opposition to the established interpretation of Israel's past and shatters the base on which his optimistic contemporaries have founded their hopes for the future.

Modern readers are accustomed to narratives composed from the perspective of the outsider: Huck Finn, Holden Caulfield, Nick Carraway, as well as such real-life outsiders as Thoreau or Malcolm X. But it is well to remember that the posture was not so familiar to the ancients. Traditional oral narrative proceeds largely on the basis of consensus. Spoken out of the heart of the community's shared experience, it is a participatory activity in which the narrator draws on a story-line and images familiar to the audience. Interest is sustained by introduction of fresh verbal formulations or variant content, but the basic perspective remains essentially unchanged through generations of recitation, and therefore this activity is one of the most important ways that the dominant cultural perspective is affirmed and perpetuated.

Adopting the position of the outsider, however, represents an important intellectual achievement. For the margins are the place of the social critic. Standing outside the main cultural arena, one can discern large patterns of thought, behavior, and value. From this distance, they can be subjected to scrutiny and judgment. Moreover, taking the position on the edge affords a new literary possibility: namely, exploiting the culture's linguistic resources from an ironic perspective, in order to disclose alternatives to common understandings. The term 'literary' is used here in a narrow sense, for it is probably only the writer who can sustain that position as a basis for communication. Writing is the medium of the committed ironist, for it enforces distance. Simply as a practical necessity, one must withdraw from other activity in order to write. But more significantly, writing introduces intellectual distance, in that it facilitates a move out of immersion in the immediate situation and encourages reflection, a kind of thinking which is analytical if not greatly abstract. A related feature of writing is its capacity to serve as an exploratory device. In comparison to the oral narrator, the writer is less constrained by the tradition and the audience's expectations. Writing affords the flexibility and wide-ranging control necessary for revealing unexpected aspects of experience and bringing them into relation (complementary or contradictory) with what was known before. Thus it commends itself to the ironist's task of probing an ideational system in search of the inherent tensions and weak points.

It is evident how, by virtue of these features, written narrative is instrumental to Ezekiel's enterprise of reconceptualizing Israel's history. By confronting Israel with this ironic inversion of the *Heilsgeschichte*, the prophet forces the people's attention away from the immediate and calls them to a task of self-evaluation on a scale never previously undertaken. Other prophets find historical grounds for divine judgment, but only Ezekiel insists upon Israel's systematic reckoning with its past as a record, first of vulnerability and dependence upon God (16.22, 43 [*Qere*]), and then of its own evil deeds (16.61, 63; 20.43; 36.31; cf. 23.45). For this prophet alone, straddling with his comprehensive vision the greatest rupture in Israelite history and struggling to render that sensible, retrospectivity is the first requirement for moral and religious development.

The depth of alienation evident in Ezekiel's narrative raises again the question of the prophet's audience treated in the last chapter. For who could hear this version of Israel's history? The pronounced marginality of the point of view expressed here confirms the impression gained elsewhere from Ezekiel's use of a restricted linguistic code: namely, that this prophecy is not intended for everyone. Ezekiel's position is from the beginning defined largely by its difference; he is commanded to distinguish himself from the rebellious majority (2.8) and warned that faithful fulfilment of his commission will win him no favor with his compatriots (2.6; 3.7). I accept the argument that the common view of Ezekiel as Israel's first great proponent of individual responsibility warrants reassessment.[25] He is still primarily concerned with the future of Israel as a corporate entity. Nonetheless, as I have already suggested, the prophet does not look for many of his contemporaries to heed his words and thus enter into that future. That this prophecy is no exhortation addressed to the masses may explain how small a part is played in it by any kind of repentance preaching.[26] Rather, Ezekiel devises a much more complex form of prophetic speech, one which is 'educational' in a quite literal sense. He uses historical narrative to lead his audience out to the margins, where they may be instructed in his perspective. Whoever wishes to understand him must move out to the place where he has taken his stand, the place from which the familiar world can be viewed with alien eyes, its patterns discerned, its values criticized. There on the margins the prophet begins to form a new community which is all the more cohesive because of the strength of the majority against which it is defined.

## Creating the Future

It is not only because it represents a critical posture that the outsider's perspective occupies an important place in literary history. Standing at a distance from received opinion also affords the opportunity for imagining new possibilities. Ezekiel calls the community which he begins to form on the edge of society, first to a rigorous process of recollection and self-examination, but then to participation in another task, which is essentially a creative one. There is an important sense in which narrative functions for Ezekiel in a way similar to the repentance preaching of other prophets: to open the gateway of hope and show the ground on which the future can be laid.

I have argued that Ezekiel's pre-fall narratives are teleologically constructed and that their point of orientation is the collapse of Jerusalem. It is their purpose to render that event historically comprehensible and theologically acceptable. The disaster is the fixed focal point for the first part of the book, and yet even there it does not mark the final horizon of Ezekiel's vision. As was seen with respect to ch. 20, the early narrative contains within it the potential of passing its first goal and becoming oriented to a new end: the establishment of a chastened and purged people in its land. The projected history of the returned people is taken up in 36.16-38, and also in the account of Gog of Magog (chs. 38-39).[27] A similar reorientation occurs at the level of the divine visions, where chs. 40-48 reverse the picture of perverted worship and divine abandonment in chs. 8-11, chronicling YHWH's return to the land and setting forth the new conditions for worship which will obtain in that epoch. It has often been noted that the series of divine visions is one of the chief marks of the book's deliberate structure. Here I wish to explore the dynamics whereby the literary device of narrative turns this textual reorientation to practical effect.

It is a question of what speech act theory calls illocutionary force. Every utterance may be understood as having both locutionary meaning, determined by its sense and reference, and illocutionary force, establishing how the utterance is to stand with respect to the interlocutors: as question, declaration, command, etc. Illocutionary force cannot always be determined on the basis of semantic or grammatical markers; one must know also something of the context of speaking, including the power relation between addresser and addressee. 'The window sill is dirty', may be an assertion of significant fact when made by a detective trying to determine where the murderer gained entrance; when spoken by householder to housekeeper, it might be either an order to clean it or a threat of dismissal. Utterances are characterized also by perlocutionary effect, the goal or result of the illocutionary act, which depends not only on the speaker's or author's intention but also on the beliefs and intentions of the audience and the circumstances of speaking. Even an utterance which itself constitutes a perlocutionary act ('I declare war', 'I baptize you in the Name of the Father, and of the Son, and of the Holy Spirit') requires acknowledgement of the speaker's authority to perform such an act under the conditions obtaining (a person baptized in a stageplay does not thereby become a member of the Church).

Much scholarly discussion concerning the Temple vision revolves around the question of its status as a speech act. One of two approaches is commonly taken. According to the first, the chief value or difficulty in the vision lies in its prescriptive force; i.e., it is exerting the illocutionary force of a command. Such a view is represented by Bertholet's influential description of the vision as a 'constitutional sketch' and has also led to the frequent and sometimes deprecating characterization of Ezekiel as the 'father of Judaism'. A similar assumption regarding the prescriptive intent of the final section of the book seems to lie behind Greenberg's surprisingly flat evaluation:

> Wherever Ezekiel's program can be checked against subsequent events it proves to have had no effect.... His program remains of interest chiefly as a practical extension of his prophecy; as additional evidence of his graphic mentality, his love of system and detail; and above all, for his lofty conception of the prophet's responsibility in an age of ruin.[28]

The second mode of reading the vision is as a purely descriptive piece. Yadin distinguishes on the grounds of intention between Ezekiel's vision report and the Qumran Temple Scroll. The first shows a divine reality, the 'Temple of the future' which God alone is one day to realize on earth. By contrast, the Essene document is found to have a programmatic significance; it actually instructs the Israelites concerning the Temple which they are to build themselves. Eichrodt also sees in chs. 40–48 the description of a building which is wholly miraculous in character and origin: 'The temple makes its appearance as a heavenly reality created by Yahweh himself and transplanted to stand on earth.... There is nothing to suggest that it should have a human builder'.[29]

But either approach leads to serious difficulties of interpretation. The prescriptive view runs into the apparent historical contradiction that Ezekiel's vision was preserved as authoritative and yet not followed as a program for reconstruction by the post-exilic community. Despite Greenberg, it is difficult to believe that the tradents and canonizers of the book judged the interest of this section only in terms of what it reveals about Ezekiel's mental habits or even his sense of responsibility—a view not easily reconciled with the theocentric tone which dominates the whole. The difficulty of the descriptive approach, on the other hand, is that it tends to make a breach between the final vision and the rest of the book, which is frankly oriented toward Israel's action—although, as I have argued, that action is in the first instance largely of a cognitive sort. Eichrodt asserts that the section is a 'self-contained whole', although, somewhat contradictorily, he then attempts to show its connection with ideas expressed elsewhere in the book.

A more subtle perspective concerning the intention of chs. 40–48 is apparent in the works of Zimmerli and Levenson, although they differ considerably on the question of authorship. Levenson adopts a conservative stance: he does not distinguish literary layers within the material and considers the bulk of the Temple vision to be Ezekiel's own. Moreover, he argues for thematic and stylistic continuity between chs. 1–39 and 40–48, finding in both a dialectical tension between divine grace and the ambivalent moral character of humankind, expressed in the interweaving of Eden and Zion traditions on the one hand and Sinai on the other. Contrary to Eichrodt, he asserts the importance of human striving, evidenced by occasional homiletic outbursts such as 45.9, and indirectly but no less significantly by the vision's specificity, which bespeaks programmatic intent. Nonetheless, Levenson recognizes that the vision exceed the bounds of human achievement:

> (Man) cannot create the waters of life (Ezek. 47:1-12), but he can build the Temple from which they issue. He cannot rebuild the Temple until he returns from Babylon, and he cannot return from Babylon unless God brings him back alive (37:21), and he cannot live unless he repents (33:14-16).[30]

Zimmerli, by contrast, details a very complex process of literary development, and he remains agnostic as to the authorship even of the basic stratum.[31] But he, too, attends to the way in which the descriptive language of the vision exerts hortatory force:

> Through the objective proclamation of the new Temple layout (*Anlage*), which includes no expressly parenetic elements, Israel, which has its old Temple and its layout in front of it, will shamefacedly recognize how it has erred in the layout of the old Temple, behind which stand a definite building concept and comprehensive notions of the Temple's arrangement and ordering. The architectural plan over which the author of xl–xlii (basic text)

bends, thus becomes in a way quite singular in the Old Testament a
document of repentance preaching.[32]

As a point of linkage between these two modes of address, 43.10-
12[33] warrants particular attention. Concluding the measuring tour of
the building,[34] it shows how the architectural description is to be
decoded into the language of faith (cf. Ps. 48.13-15). Like the
conclusions to the narrative histories in Chs. 16 and 20, this passage
affirms the connection between new vision and memory, between
restoration and repentance.[35] The Temple vision speaks in the most
concrete terms of YHWH's intention for Israel, which enables both a
responsible turning to the past and a hopeful movement into the
future. In view of this enabling intention, I cannot agree with
Levenson's comment (following upon that cited above) that 'To ask
which came first, grace or works, is like asking about the chicken and
the egg'.[36] The extent of the disaster reveals Israel's powerlessness to
initiate its own restoration; the depth of its sin destroys any illusion
of an equal partnership with God. Nonetheless, the way in which the
vision is set forth anticipates and requires the people's participation
(note the explicitly volitive language of 43.7-9 and the plural
formation, ומדדו את-תכנית 'and let them measure the design', v. 10).
Moreover, the designation תורת הבית (v. 12) for the vision as a whole
is an unambiguous indicator of its illocutionary force. The Temple
plan is commanded as much as revealed; Israel should not only take
the building's measure but also actively observe (וישמרו v. 11) its form
and laws, and perform them.

Earlier I suggested that the activity of narrating is a chief, even
essential component of the process whereby we construct and learn
to maneuver in hypothetical worlds. This would seem to offer insight
into the relation between the descriptive and the prescriptive
elements of Ezekiel's vision report. Both may be seen as aspects of
the way the narrative accomplishes its aim, which is perhaps best
described as 'world-creating'.[37] It is not due to its fictional status that
a work might warrant this ascription, but rather by virtue of its
intention toward the audience: to invite imaginative participation in
alternative modes of reality, which open up new understandings and
possibilities for our existence simply by virtue of their difference
from immediate experience. Modal indicators (e.g. 43.7-9; 45.9) are
only one way that a narrative might convey such an intention. More
significant is the context in which the narrative is promulgated.

Certainly prophetic speech, whose whole purpose is to expose the wide discrepancy between the real and the ideal and in different ways to effect an orientation or movement toward the latter, is such a context. And surely written narrative, with its plasticity, organizational scope, and especially the time for reflection which it affords both author and reader, is an efficacious means for the creation of new worlds.[38]

One of the peculiar features of the Temple vision is the fact that it does not mention the sanctuary walls—a strange economy in a description otherwise so full. The common explanation is that Ezekiel was working from, even meditating on a blueprint, which accounts for both the precision of his measurements and the fact that he confines his vision to a groundplan.[39] But the explanation is inadequate. Granted that the Temple plan is plausibly based on a previously outlined program for reconstruction, still that does not determine the nature of the prophet's conception or circumscribe its scope. Perhaps, as Zimmerli suggests, he did prepare a drawing for his audience; whether or not this is the case, Zimmerli's reading of וכתב in 43.11 as 'draw' misses what is at most an ambiguous reference (cf. חקק in 4.1, 23.14) and fails to account for the inclusion of the non-visual pair תורות-חוקות ('laws-statutes', cf. 44.5) in the items to be recorded.[40] Ezekiel communicated God's revelation to Israel as prophets always had: with words, this time prepared in writing.[41] The text which the prophet produced has its own expressive range, independent of any document which may have inspired it, and it is the effect of this text which should be registered. The vision report must be acknowledged for what it is: a dynamic narrative, the result of a complex creative process, which is itself conducive to further creativity on the part of those to whom it is addressed.

It is logical, then, to assume that the absence of any reference to the walls is an omission meaningful within the context of the present narrative. And the most obvious inference to be drawn is that Ezekiel wanted to show a Temple still under construction. Zimmerli suggests that the date of the Temple vision (40.1) marks the halfway point to the Jubilee, the great fiftieth year of release, a concept to which the exile gave new significance (cf. Isa. 61.1-9); and the fact that the number twenty-five and its multiples dominate the measurements which follow adds substance to his case.[42] It would seem that the whole structure of the vision is anticipatory, that the Temple is not represented as accomplished fact, even in the divine realm; Israel must wait, and probably also work, for the accomplishment of this blessing.[43] The very incompleteness of the description exerts a kind of directive force toward Ezekiel's audience to participate in the vision's fulfilment.

Almost all commentators (excepting Greenberg) consider that the diversity of perspectives found in the present form of the Temple vision is best explained as the result of several editorial hands, probably including that of the original author.[44] The approach taken here, unlike Greenberg's holistic method, is not undercut by acknowledging such development. Rather, the way in which narrative invites embellishment is one of its pronounced features. Taking advantage of that invitation is an obvious and highly prized feature of oral narrative performance. But written narrative, too, is susceptible to elaboration—a fact of which modern copyright laws and the whole concept of a literary work as the private creation of an individual have suppressed our awareness. This follows quite naturally from two factors: first, the relative openness of narrative style (in contrast with that of lyric poetry), which admits of amplification without disturbance of the basic structure; and second, its selectivity, the fact that narrative always leaves gaps for the imagination to fill. Indeed, since the act of reading a narrative always entails an inferential process of filling in its gaps, the only question, in any given instance, is how far-reaching this imaginative act will be, and whether it will be formalized into a new text.

A conception of individual authorship gradually established itself in the ancient world but in Israel, at least, never became an exclusive one. It was a mark of honor to a master and, more importantly, an extension of his authority for disciples to add their words to his without noting the distinction. The prophetic corpus certainly offers abundant evidence of this process of slipping—without intention to deceive— later writings (ranging in length from a few verses to the many chapters of exilic and restoration period 'Isaiahs') under the outstretched mantle. The fact that Ezekiel appears to have been the first of the canonical writers to sign his work (1.1) did not inhibit that process. Rather, precisely because of the 'elevated prose' style which dominates the whole, his book seems to have been particularly susceptible to amplification.[45]

Within the Temple vision, the narrative development seems to display several different tendencies or, one could say, to be a response to pressure of various kinds. In some instances, amplification is apparently prompted by a desire for logical completeness. 41.5-15a[46] supplies information about the exterior dimensions of the Temple and its outlying western building that did not fit into the basic guided tour, which follows an interior route leading to the Holy of Holies. Or the addition may serve a harmonizing function: 45.1-5 mediates between the provision for priestly and levitical allotments in ch. 48, and the prohibition on such allotments in 44.28. The vision also attracts additions (e.g., the regulations concerning the prince and the specification of weights and measures) aimed at providing a broader picture of life in the resettled community.

A particularly interesting example of narrative development occurs in 44.6-31. While the section recalls the rhetoric of chs. 1–24 in its condemnation of the house of Israel as 'rebellious' (מרי, v. 6), it differs in making an explicit exception of the Zadokites. Zimmerli correctly notes that the style of personal address to Israel is significant: 'The desire to formulate a judgment oracle in the prophetic style can be clearly discerned even if subsequently the power to carry it through is lacking'.[47] However, he does not really show why this has happened, or wherein lies the new power of speech. The judgment oracle is swallowed up by the narrative: a faltering is evident already in the appearance of a third-person verbal form (ויפרו)[48] in v. 7, and by v. 10 the assimilation is complete.

The important factor in this abandonment of personal address is what written discourse does and does not do well. Unlike living speech, it does not make its impact in a shattering moment of direct confrontation. Writing has a cumulative effect; it builds its case through the amassing and ordering of evidence and the delineation of consequences. The narratives of chs. 16, 20, and 23 accomplish this in the realm of history (though retaining in large part the form of personal address); the Temple vision, in terms of the architecture and ritual of the cult. The force of a direct invective would be greatly vitiated by this careful structure, which, more than any other part of the book, demands attention specifically as a text.[49] So, rather than mounting an assault on the conscience, the author of this passage plants an expression of disapprobation designed to provoke the reflective imagination. The form of condemnation appropriate within this exquisitely differentiated system is to show what diminished status the Levites' deeds have earned them and, by contrast, to assert the privileges of the Zadokites.

Finally, I wish to acknowledge the limits of the argument presented here. I have tried to show how narrative theory is useful in illumining certain fundamental features of Ezekiel's prophecy. This should not be confused with a proposal that the book be treated as a narrative whole, in which (ideally) all elements contribute to a single line of development. While demonstrating an organizational structure broader and tighter than that of any previous prophetic writing, it obviously lacks the comprehensive, closely sequential design of a modern narrative work, either fictional or historical. Moreover, many individual passages remain close to the inherited forms of oracular speech. Ezekiel's achievement is in making narrative a vehicle of prophecy, not in converting all prophetic speech into narrative. But neither the prophet nor the argument for the centrality of narrative should be faulted on that account. Indeed, this is appropriate: for, though he may be a 'writing prophet' unlike any other, what Ezekiel produces must nevertheless be recognizable *as prophecy* by the exiles. The success of the enterprise depends upon his maintaining a balance between utilizing new opportunities and creating something comprehensible to those still thinking in old categories. How far he succeeded in effecting permanent change in the idiom of prophecy will be taken up in the next chapter.

## Chapter 6

## CHARTING A FUTURE FOR PROPHECY

Tout graphème est d'essence testamentaire (Jacques Derrida, *De la grammatologie*).

### *Stranger among the Prophets*

The preceding chapters have treated some of the distinctive features of Ezekiel's prophecy, features which, not coincidentally, have constituted the chief critical problems of the book. My task has not been primarily an exegetical one; in only one instance, the figure of the prophet's dumbness, have I suggested a substantially new reading. Rather, it has been to outline a mode of intepretation. I have employed a theory of written discourse to show that these problematic features are best understood as aspects of Ezekiel's effort to create a new literary idiom for prophecy. He develops an archival speech form which is oriented less toward the immediate press of events in the political sphere than toward reformation of the tradition in light of the catastrophic event of Jerusalem's fall, an event which gave the lie to the prevailing self-laudatory interpretations of Israel's sacred history. Furthermore, if Ezekiel is, like earlier prophets, a public figure, nevertheless he has taken a step back from direct confrontation with an audience as the essential dynamic of prophetic communication. He formulates his speech in such a way as to facilitate a kind of engagement whose essential medium is not the person of the prophet but the text.

These observations about how Ezekiel reshapes prophetic discourse as a form of social interaction suggest that a reevaluation of Ezekiel's place in the history of prophecy is in order. Critical regard for his contribution to the prophetic tradition has generally been low. Wellhausen asserted outright that genuine prophecy ended with

Jeremiah. Ezekiel is no more than an clever imitator, slipping his primarily priestly concerns under the authoritative mantle of prophecy. He is the first of the *epigoni*, who meditate and comment on the words of the old prophets rather than producing any fresh revelation.[1] Although Blenkinsopp hesitates to apply that label, his recent evaluation does not differ in substance: '[Ezekiel] is the first to exhibit clearly in his work the collapse of propheticism into priestly and scribal forms'.[2] And even Heschel, whose perspective on such matters may be assumed to owe relatively little to Wellhausen, tacitly affirms his judgment that Ezekiel does not really belong among Israel's prophets; of the major prophetic works, only Ezekiel's receives no substantial attention in Heschel's theological investigation of prophecy.[3] A more subtle way of undermining his status as a prophet has been to emphasize, not what has ended, but the new phase of Israelite religion which begins with Ezekiel. So there have emerged genealogical theories which hail him variously as the father of 'apocalyptic' or founder of Judaism, pioneer of personal religion or speculative theology in Israel.

Scholars whose work is in large part devoted to this book have not been inclined, at least in recent years, to share the negative estimation of the prophet *qua* prophet. Yet they have done very little to counter it. As the preceding study indicates, the tendency has been to minimize or ignore the difference between Ezekiel and his predecessors. Zimmerli's essentially form-critical approach is based on an assumption that the same categories which have proved fruitful for investigation of classical prophecy are applicable, with modification, here. While Greenberg traces elaborate patterns which would seem to suggest that very different conventions have come into play for the composition and appropriation of prophecy, he makes no attempt to coordinate his distinctively literary mode of analysis with observations concerning how this kind of language must have functioned in a social setting. Although Lang does directly take up the question of the prophet's social role, it is with the aim of showing that Ezekiel is still operating within a political framework— a notion which, as I have argued, is untenable on several grounds.[4]

The attempt to secure Ezekiel's place among the prophets by underplaying his strangeness is misguided. The whole purpose of this study has been to show that something radically different does begin with Ezekiel. If it is too much to set him, as Wellhausen does, outside of prophecy, yet a proper appreciation of his position entails recognition that with him, prophecy undergoes a shift of major social significance. Ezekiel is the pivotal figure in the movement which was, paradoxically, both to mark the 'end' of prophecy and to establish its permanence as a source of authority in Israel.

### The Way of Transformation

The shape of the Hebrew Bible encourages the perception that the creative epoch of Israelite prophecy ended with the exile. The period in which new prophetic sayings were preserved and promulgated as independent collections began to draw to a close; among the books of the Israelite prophets, probably only Joel is to be dated more than a century after the return. The view is widespread that prophecy expired under the pressure of a host of external forces which, playing upon its internal tensions, became intolerable under Babylonian and Persian rule. Recent scholarship has offered several suggestions concerning the factors underlying the decline of prophecy. Cross stresses the intimate relation between the office of the king and that of the prophet, whose function was as much political as religious; therefore, when Israel ceased to be a self-determining nation, prophecy became otiose.[5] Blenkinsopp notes as a factor closely related to the loss of royal patronage the contact with Babylonian scholarship, with its reverence for the written word and the wisdom of the past over the spoken word and fresh inspirations.[6]

Ideological factors are put forth as having hastened the demise of prophecy. Crenshaw maintains that the prophets' job of asserting the will of YHWH in interventionist fashion was rendered superfluous by the post-exilic theocracy, which was already seen to be the institutional fulfillment of the divine will. Furthermore, prophecy could not bear the burden of history; it proved too inflexible to bridge the disparity between Israel's faith and its confused and bitter experience. The tragedy of prophecy was that it failed to assert, in an atmosphere in which the doubts of the people were fed by delayed fulfilment and conflicting oracles of hope and doom, any criterion by which the true word of God might be known.[7] Therefore Israel turned increasingly to other forms of religious expression—wisdom, apocalyptic—whose valdity was less perceptibly connected with the exercise of power and the outcome of events in the immediate historical sphere.

It is almost certain that all of the external factors mentioned here played a part in the change which occurred in prophecy, i.e., that prophecy's 'failure' was overdetermined and correspondingly rapid. But I wish to reexamine this radical change in Israel's religious ideology from a somewhat different perspective: namely, to focus on the extent to which accommodation was made while still maintaining an identity that was distinctly prophetic. Viewed from this perspective, I think it can be shown that the prophets did not simply dwindle away in the face of adversity. Instead, they participated actively in transformation of their own social role—though perhaps unmindful of the full consequences—and thereby saved themselves from oblivion.[8]

It is not accurate to say simply that during and after the exile, prophecy was found to be irrelevant, and therefore its influence declined. This is the situation which demands explanation: at the same time that the activity of current prophets was gradually ceasing to be ratified through the circulation of stories and speeches bearing their names, there was an increasing tendency to look to the recorded sayings of earlier prophets. Their prestige was enhanced through amplification and editing of their writings, a process which served both to fill out the story of the past (e.g., the prose additions to the book of Jeremiah) and also to carry forward the tradition, renewing and modifying its themes in light of a changed situation (as happened to the prophecies of Isaiah). The crucial point is that, while the person of the *prophet* as an identifiable contemporary figure was becoming less important, even contemptible (Jer. 23.34-40;[9] Zech. 13.2-6), the phenomenon of *prophecy* itself, construed as a mode of authoritative speech deeply rooted in if not belonging exclusively to the nation's past, was gaining in significance as it solidified into a permanent repository of texts.

This reorientation from prophecy as a current mode of activity to prophecy as a written record is sometimes attributed to the fact that the practice of prophecy was on the wane. Blenkinsopp refers to a 'decline in the quality of official, public prophecy' between the first and second deportations to Babylon and cites as evidence Jer. 29.8; Ezek. 13.7-9, 23; 22.8.[10] Wilson considers the change in quantitative terms: 'Because the prophets were becoming rare, the [support] groups seem to have turned to the prophetic literature, which they had helped to preserve....'[11] But if it was indeed the case that prophetic activity had deteriorated, firm evidence is lacking. The prophets' own polemical statements cannot be taken as such evidence; were they seriously regarded in this way, then Ezekiel's denial that anyone stood in the breach on Israel's behalf (22.30) would invalidate Jeremiah's efforts. Moreover, the cynical representations in post-exilic texts indicate that prophecy was not so rare as to have ceased to be problematic. Whatever may have been the actual state of prophetic practice in post-exilic Israel, it can be said with certainty that the view which achieved canonical status was that the great era of prophetic pronouncements had passed.[12] This view prevailed so strongly that even some who stood in the line of succession seem to have regarded their own stature as diminished in comparison with that of past prophets (cf. Zech. 1.4-6; 7.7).

Crucial to understanding this situation is an appreciation of literary activity as an instrument of social change and not merely a means of reflecting its occurrence. Earlier I discussed the way in which the process of inscription affects the dynamics of communication. By virtue of their relative autonomy from the circumstances of their origin, texts invite reinterpretation and reapplication to new situations to a far greater extent than does living speech. Therefore it is not necessary or perhaps even valid to assume that contemporary prophecy had degenerated to the point that the community was forced to rely on the words of the past. It may be, in fact, that the causality operated instead or simultaneously in the reverse direction: that the existence of the prophetic literature created a wealth of hermeneutical possibilities which lessened the need to legitimate new oracles and thus led to a devaluation of present practice.[13]

Actually, there are aspects of the critical discussion which would support the view that the inscription of prophecy preceded and contributed to its eclipse as a contemporary phenomenon. Such a perception may inform Wellhausen's judgment that Ezekiel cannot really be reckoned a prophet at all: 'Ezekiel had swallowed a book (iii. 1-3), and gave it out again'.[14] With respect to this view, particular attention must be paid to Blenkinsopp's argument that the shift to emphasis on the prophetic literature results from the tension between prophecy and scribalism as conflicting hermeneutical traditions, the first standing 'for openness in relating tradition and situation',[15] the second for the maintenance of normative order based on the law. According to his argument, the progressive canonization of prophecy appears largely as a scribal victory. The power of the prophets is first regulated and then in a sense neutralized by respectfully 'kicking them upstairs'. Now memorialized in writing, prophecy is accorded the status of an honorable institution belonging to a former dispensation.

There is some truth to this claim. The first important step in relegating prophecy to the past is the Deuteronomic criterion for identifying a false oracle: the word which does not come to pass has been spoken presumptuously, without genuine divine inspiration (Deut. 18.21-22). Since the criterion can only be applied retrospectively, the question of the authoritative status of new oracles must be bracketed. It is, then, no longer the immediate impact of prophet upon audience which counts. Whatever significance prophecy is perceived to have derives from it only as a corpus of sayings whose validity has been proven in the (shorter or longer) course of history.

What I would question, however, is the extent to which this movement toward textualization really reflects a tension between the prophets and the legal specialists, and the triumph of the latter. It seems likely that in the late monarchy and the exilic period, the two groups were dealing with many of the same problems and devising similar solutions. The passage just cited from Deuteronomy shows, in fact, how close they were. The prophets were as passionately concerned as the Deuteronomic scribes to validate the true word of God; and both Jeremiah and Ezekiel—although under different circumstances and at different stage in their careers—produced a permanent record of their predictions, a record which could be consulted after the time of fulfillment and thus retrospectively validate the divine commission to prophesy. As I have argued, the existence of a permanently divided community made writing as indispensable to the exilic prophets as it had long been to those who transmitted the legal and narrative traditions. Further, the prophets and their students, no less than the scribes, felt the need for consolidating the tradition and reinterpreting the past following the successive devastations of the Northern Kingdom (evidenced, for example, in the reworking of the message of Hosea to include Judah) and Judah.[16] I have tried to show that the thoroughgoing fashion in which Ezekiel pursues this task requires the critical distance and the control over large bodies of material which writing facilitates.

Finally, it must be noted that Ezekiel himself seems not to be aware of, let alone traumatized by, the 'unresolved tension' which Blenkinsopp perceives between Law and Prophets as representing different hermeneutics of the tradition.[17] He uses the language of both spheres freely and in a way which is mutually reinforcing. The clearest instance is ch. 18, where Ezekiel treats the prophetic theme of repentance within the context of a legal disquisition. The effect of their combination is consonant with the purposes of the priestly pedagogue: thus he extends the horizon of the people's concern beyond the immediate situation and educates them for the future. Yet Ezekiel shows the sensibility of the prophet in setting one of his rare direct summonses (v. 30) at the end of the long theoretical discussion, where it greatly heightens the existential force of the rhetoric.

I would, then, agree with Blenkinsopp that there is a crucial connection between, on the one hand, the creation of a corpus of prophetic literature and, on the other, the fact that prophecy as a contemporary phenomenon sunk in official esteem. I would further agree that explication of this connection touches on the most important religious developments in exilic and post-exilic Israel. Where I depart from him is in maintaining that what came to be the official position reflects not only scribal interests but also the concerns of the prophets and their own attempts to meet the new challenges to communication in the sixth and fifth centuries. In other words, the change which occurs in the way prophecy is pursued and perceived should be regarded largely as an inner transformation, occurring in response to external pressures and also to some degree in conjunction with similar changes in other spheres, notably the legal one.

## The Disappearing Prophet

I have already noted that the essential phenomenon in this transformation of prophecy is the shift in emphasis from the person of the prophet to the words ascribed to the prophet, which have been given permanent and authoritative form in the text. In order to understand the nature of this shift, it is necessary to coordinate it more closely with the notion, implicit in a theory of written discourse, that the effect of writing is to separate speech not only from the circumstances of its origin but also from the person of the originator. It could be said that with the inscription of discourse, a reversal takes place in the generative relation between speaker and speech. Once the literary work has assumed independent existence, the writer (viewed from the perspective of the text) becomes unimportant, even disappears as an historically distinct individual, replaced by the 'implied author', a fictitious person who is not creator but creation, a function of the work itself. The extent of the separation between author and work is potentially such that post-structuralist critics have become accustomed to speak of the text as implying the death of the writer.[18]

A process of objectifying prophetic speech is, as I have noted, already evident when Jeremiah encounters and consumes YHWH's words (15.16). The independent status of the inscribed word is underscored in ch. 36, of which von Rad observes:

> The story is unique in the Old Testament, since its subject is neither a person, nor an act of Jahweh's providence or appointment, but a book. But the book's fortunes epitomise the fortunes of the message it contained. Once more the *motif* is that of the great failure, which Jeremiah plays with his own particular variations. We might therefore almost speak of a 'passion' undergone by the book as well as by its author. At one point, however, the parallel with Jeremiah's own *via dolorosa* breaks down. The scroll is torn and burnt, but it is renewed. Jahweh's word does not allow itself to be brought to naught.[19]

The final qualification is crucial for the direction which prophecy would take. The possibility of permanence proved a decisive advantage for the inscribed word, and this ramified directly to the representation of the prophet. It is only with Jeremiah and, to a lesser degree, Habakkuk (ch. 1)[20] that the prophetic 'I' becomes a subject of independent interest, asserting itself strongly in challenge to YHWH's will (excepting the late book of Jonah, where the difference in perspective is evident from the fact that the rebellious prophet is reduced to a caricature). As I have argued, Ezekiel, far from emerging as a distinct personality defining himself through complaint and reproach directed against God, appears rather as the almost transparent vessel of the divine word. While von Rad is certainly right that Ezekiel shows his 'modernity' in developing a novel viewpoint over against the tradition, he is hardly (contrary to von

Rad) an individual in the same sense as Jeremiah.[21] The latter represents the acme and the end of the attempt to render the prophetic persona as a recognizable self. Zimmerli is much closer to the mark with his admission that 'Ezekiel's personality is hidden by stylized forms and traditions more deeply than any other of the great prophetic figures'.[22] The prophet who swallowed the scroll becomes (to our eyes, at least) virtually indistinguishable from what he ate. Adapting his speech to the form of a permanent record, the person of the speaker recedes behind the stability and prominence of the concretized word.

In its next and final appearance within the prophetic literature (Zech. 5.1-4), the figure of the scroll shows a further marked progression in the eclipse of the prophet as being himself a source of powerful speech. Zechariah watches the flying scroll swoop overhead and learns from the angelic interpreter about its mission of destruction. The scroll is itself the agent of YHWH's will, the written word inexplicably active in the world to punish the lawless. The prophet does not eat or read or even touch it; there is no indication that he is to exercise any function with respect to the scroll or its mission. This form of the figure reveals the extent to which the inscribed word has been rendered independent of the person of the prophet.

The representation of Zechariah throughout the first part of the book (chs. 1-8) shows that the function of the prophet has undergone a development which is, if not exactly surprising in light of the lines laid down by Ezekiel, nonetheless striking. Here the problem of identifying a setting for his public activity becomes quite insoluble. The superscription gives no location for the revelation (1.1; contrast Ezek. 1.1); there is no indication either of the audience for which this prophecy was intended or that any of it was ever delivered.[23] Moreover, the material is only in small part formulated as actual proclamation (1.3-7, 14-17; 7.4-7; and the collection of sayings in ch. 8; cf. such anomalies as 2.8b-17, in oracular form yet addressed by an angel to the 'young man' without instruction to proclaim it publicly, and 7.8-14, where an exhortation of the people is juxtaposed with a narrative concerning them). Rapid alternations between first- and third-person references to the prophet (e.g. 7.1, 4, 8) show that there is no longer a fixed convention for the presentation of prophetic speech. The 'autobiographical' style introduced by Ezekiel seems to have exercised some influence, although the traditional third-person perspective has not been relinquished. As I have argued, experimentation with perspective most probably reflects a situation in which prophecy has become largely a matter of written composition.

As part of the move whereby Ezekiel renounces the role of mediator in a two-way interaction between God and the people, he casts himself in the role of first listener and model respondent to what is effectively a divine monologue. This theocentric reorientation of discourse is the crucial step whereby the figure of the prophet becomes dispensable within the process of communication. When the primary task is merely one of reliable transmission, a task which is best consigned to writing, it is not surprising that the figure of the prophet should become increasingly attenuated and in some cases disappear altogether as an entity independent of the text. In addition, this reorientation represents a move toward the transcendentalization of prophecy; it emphasizes the utter disparity between YHWH as the sole originator of speech and all humans, whose only real choice is whether to listen or not, but not how to answer back.

Zechariah takes this move a degree further. He, too, is not mediator but listener; but more than that, his experience of hearing the divine word is itself mediated by heavenly beings. North points to the vitality which the account draw from interaction between the prophet and these angels, and among the angels themselves.[24] But probably the more pertinent point is that this interaction takes the place of any direct involvement with an audience as the dynamic which generates this prophecy. Whatever it means for Zechariah to be a prophet, his commission does not seem to entail any immediate obligation with respect to his contemporaries. Indeed, one of the divine beings usurps from him the book's only faint echo of a mediator's function, the protest against divine judgment spoken on Israel's behalf (Zech. 1.12; contrast Ezek. 11.13).

On the one side, then, this prophecy testifies to the growing perception of an unbridgeable gulf between the divine and the human worlds, one which finally separates even the prophet from YHWH. Though Ezekiel knew God to be impassible to any fulminations from his side, still he felt the force of YHWH's hand in the most vivid way: feeding him (3.2), seizing him by the hair and transporting him 'between the earth and the sky' to Jerusalem (8.3). But Zechariah experiences no direct contact; he only hears a voice and sees visions—and not transparent manifestations of YHWH's glory, such as Ezekiel sees, but symbolical abstractions which magnify the distance between divine reality and human comprehension, visions whose significance emerges only through angelic interpretation.

On the other side, there is a separation between Zechariah and his contemporaries, those who would presumably constitute his audience. This style of prophecy is obviously the product of reflection, on earlier prophecy as well as on Zechariah's own visions,[25] and it demands to be received on the same terms. There is little which adheres to the genres associated with live speech or appears to be designed for direct impact. Robert North comments:

> The artificiality and structure of First-Zechariah's visions, with their interpreting angels, suggest that we have here a literary composition intended to be read silently rather than aloud. This is in common with the erudite apocalypts as against the oral disconnectness of what has been gathered into the 'book-'prophets.[26]

Both aspects of the prophet's separation—from YHWH and from an immediate audience—testify to a situation in which the prophet is rapidly being excluded from participation in live discourse and becoming submerged within the world of the text. Zechariah provides an interesting case study because its semi-autobiographical style does indeed seem to offer a representation of the prophet, making it easy to overlook the actual paucity of information about his person or function. But, moving back in time, we come to another prophet, this one so effectively refined out of independent existence that we do not even know a name, or see a distinct figure. All we have is a text, appended to and drawing its inspiration from another text, the work of the eighth-century Isaiah. While with Zechariah the prophetic role of mediator is appropriated by the angel interpreter, the Second Isaiah's task of proclamation would seem to be assumed by the 'evangel Zion' (מבשרת ציון, 40.9) herself.[27] That the call narrative in this text does not refer to its author, but rather to the personified people, or a portion of the nation, is a strong indication of how far the prophet's function has become detached from historically identifiable individuals.

It is a datum of common sense, but one which bears emphasis, that prophecy can only be anonymous when it is initially circulated in writing. Koch sees this convention—in which follow the Third Isaiah

and the Second (and Third?) Zechariah, and possibly Malachi, if that
designation be rendered as an appellative ('my messenger') rather
than a proper name[28]—as a return to the 'normal literary usage' of
the ancient Near East. He suggests as a possible cause a decline in
prophetic self-confidence or an interest in future predictions separated
from a particular moment in history.[29] While the second of these
explanations may represent a trend in late Israelite prophecy, already
adumbrated in Ezekiel (e.g. chs. 38–39), it is not generally applicable
to the Second Isaiah (41.2-3; 43.14; 45.1-7); and the first is hardly
more compatible with the strong tone of assurance which is precisely
what makes that prophecy so moving. It is better to offer the
observation—if not a full explanation—which draws least upon
unprovable assumptions about the disposition of the prophets, as
individuals or as a group. The fact is that it was only in the exile and
the Persian Period that the prophets were truly 'authors', conceiving
their prophecy as written works, and therefore this was the first time
that the option for anonymity existed. If anonymous composition
represented a literary norm in the culture, nonetheless it must be
recognized as something quite new for prophecy, and as effecting a
fundamental shift in this mode of authoritative speech. Henceforth,
prophecy—at least in its official, proto-canonical form—was not an
ongoing dialogue between God and Israel, turning on the person of
the prophet, but an encounter with the divine word as it was fixed in
the text.[30] New prophetic texts, even those which were not
anonymous, were generated in response to older ones, reread in the
light of present circumstances.[31] But the rapidity with which
anonymous prophecy came to be conventional shows the extent to
which prophecy had already become an exegetical enterprise carried
out among scholarly traditionists.

This shift within the prophets' self-representation suggests that
the relation between the prophets and the scribes should be seen in
terms not of competition or collapse, but rather of continuity and
succession. For the word of YHWH, though no longer embedded in a
concrete situation of live interaction, still stood in need of mediation.
The act of inscription necessitates repeated further acts of interpretation
if the text is to remain alive and be rendered useful. Without the
specifications afforded by a speaker and an immediately apparent
'spoken about', the meaning of written discourse is frustratingly,
temptingly open. Therefore, as the person of the prophet was ever

more effaced by the text, it was quite natural that the space between the word of YHWH and Israel should come to be filled by a new group of specialists, whose task it was to preserve and also to interpret—the two acts never being fully separate—the textual tradition.

This work of the scribes was far from pedestrian. In Israel, the activity of those who expounded Scripture was viewed as being almost as arcane as that of the prophets themselves, requiring a gift of fresh inspiration. Coming at the very end of the formative period for the Hebrew Bible, the book of Daniel develops this theme of inspired interpretation. The first story of Nebuchadnezzar's dream (ch. 2) shows it to be a sort of revelatory experience; a vision in the night enables Daniel to meet the king's humanly impossible demand for the interpretation of a dream whose content he will not disclose. The implication is one that post-structuralists would approve: that every interpretation is itself a new creative act, which in some sense determines the text it purports to explicate. This notion is underscored by the story of Belshazzar's feast (ch. 5), where again Daniel must effectively create the text, written in some script which only he can decipher, before offering an interpretation.

Furthermore, the interpreter of Scripture required divine guidance not just because the enterprise was difficult, but also because, as with prophecy, the stakes were high. Daniel speaks his interpretations at the risk of his life (2.18), and the reward for illumining the text is political power, which enables him to promote the safety and influence of other Jews as well as himself (2.48-49). This story, like the description of the scholar in Sir. 39.1-11, suggest the significance that during the Second Temple period attached to the work of interpretation *as a form of public service*. It was the chief intellectual activity by which the community sustained itself.[32] Through searching the Scriptures, the accumulated record of YHWH's words and actions directed toward Israel,[33] the community achieved an informed perspective on problems of its contemporary existence.

By rendering authoritative speech independent of the person of the speaker, Ezekiel set prophecy on a course from which it never turned back. Within mainstream Judaism, the person of the prophet did not again emerge as primary mediator and manipulator of the word of God. It is impossible to say whether Ezekiel consciously anticipated this development; certainly he prepared the ground for it. In creating a literary idiom for prophecy, he took a decisive step toward forging a community which defined itself on the basis of a common text and shared habits of reading. Resisting the temptation to enter directly into the heated fray which surrounded YHWH's word in the midst of Israel's greatest crisis, he gave those who would attend to him a new disposition for hearing. He began to teach Israel to listen for the authoritative word, not just in single sharp moments of revelation and confrontation, but as it would reecho through the ongoing murmur, not infrequently rising to a clamor, of centuries of interpretation.

# NOTES

## Notes to Chapter 1

1. These visions are marked as interrelated, not only by their common designation, מראות אלהים (1.1; 8.3; 40.2), but also by a continuity of motifs and structural elements, which other scholars have noted in detail. Although Parunak's attempt to show a chiastic structure within each vision and correspondence among them is not at all points convincing, his study is useful in illustrating elements of a conscious literary design running throughout. An interesting aspect of Greenberg's discussion of the relation between chs. 1 and 10 is the application of a principle previously identified by Moshe Seidel: the inversion of elements as a sign of literary reference in Scripture (*Ezekiel*, 1.198). Talmon devotes considerable attention to the visions in his efforts to establish the principles by which Ezekiel worked as both author and editor, arranging his own words for maximum effect as well as to incorporate set pieces, such as Talmon takes the plan of the Temple building to be ('Literary Structuring', 325-26).

2. *Der Prophet Ezechiel*, xxii.

3. Contrast the view of Edouard Reuss: '. . . there is not, in this whole book, a single page which we should suppose to have been read or uttered publicly. Ezekiel was not an orator; he is a writer. What he has given us are literary lucubrations, the product of study, the fruit of recollection and contemplation' (*La Bible, Traduction Nouvelle* [Paris: Sandoz et Fischbacher, 1876], *Les Prophètes* 2.10).

4. *Introduction to the Literature of the Old Testament* (New York: Charles Scribner's Sons, 1913), 279.

5. *Die Profeten* (Leipzig: Hinrichs, 1914) and *Geschichte der israelitischen und jüdischen Religion* (Giessen: Töpelmann, 1922) preceded publication of Hölscher's 1924 commentary. It should be noted that, before the tools for critical biblical study were fully available, Georg Ludwig Oeder (1756) was the first to cast doubt on the book's unity. He contended that chs. 40–48 constituted the second of two books attributed to Ezekiel by Josephus and that (contrary to Josephus) it was not his genuine creation. The work was published posthumously by Georg Vogel (*Freye Untersuchung über einige Bücher des Alten Testaments*, 1771).

6. *Hesekiel*, 5.

7. Of later studies, Irwin's (1943) most closely approaches Hölscher's method and conclusions. Starting from the parable of the useless vine in ch. 15, he identifies the interpretation (vv. 6-8) as 'false commentary' which misses the essential point of the vine's inherent worthlessness and concentrates instead on the damage inflicted by fire. On the basis, then, of the differing 'mental types' of Ezekiel and the later writers (evidencing itself in their respectively clear and discursive styles), the poetry/prose distinction (*pace* Hölscher), and the assumption that the prophet's words are properly interpreted and developed in only one direction, he goes on to distinguish original and spurious material throughout the book. All of these assumptions are unproven and impose a very restrictive standard of literary homogeneity. Certainly many modern works demonstrate a diversity of style exceeding that which Irwin allows Ezekiel; there is no reason to suppose ancient authors confined their creativity within such a narrow range. Irwin's work has had little impact on scholarly discussion.

8. Cf. *Mekilta*, Pisḥa 1: תדע שאין השכינה נגלית בחוצה לארץ ('You may know that the Shekinah does not reveal itself outside the Holy Land' [from Jonah 1.3]').

9. Otto R. Fischer, 'The Unity of the Book of Ezekiel', unpublished dissertation (Boston University, 1939).

10. Robert H. Pfeiffer, *Introduction to the Old Testament* (New York: Harper, 1941), 537-40.

11. The idea that the book was an historical fiction (of the Persian period) had been put forth more than a century before by Leopold Zunz (*Die gottesdienstlichen Vorträge der Juden*, Berlin: A. Asher, 1832), who rested his view on linguistic study, with particular emphasis on the Aramaizing element in the text.

12. *Book of the Prophet Ezekiel*, 98.

13. One notable exception is the work of Garscha (1974), promoting a view which in various forms dominated Ezekiel scholarship from Hölscher to Torrey: viz., that the book in its present form owes little if anything to the sixth-century figure. While acknowledging that the Ezekiel tradition originated with the actual prophet, Garscha considers that any genuine historical memory has been obliterated or disguised by a lengthy redactional process. One can, therefore, speak with assurance only about the effect of the present text, whose layered form has been determined by theological concerns stretching over three centuries (ending c. 300).

14. *Ezekiel*, 1.30.

15. *Ibid.*, 1.37.

16. 'All that which is preached by the prophet as an event which is apparently neutral in its meaning has its purpose in that Israel and the nations should come to a recognition, which in the Old Testament also always means an acknowedgement, of this person who reveals himself in his

name. All Yahweh's action which the prophet proclaims serves as a proof of Yahweh among the nations' (*ibid.*, 1.38).

17. Thus, for example, he distinguishes between ch. 43 and the more studied material in chs. 40–42 (*ibid.*, 2.412-13).

18. *Ibid.*, 1.71.

19. *Ibid.*, 1.68.

20. *Prophecy in Ancient Israel*, 147.

21. *Literary and Psychological Aspects*, 88.

22. *Mystikens psykologi* (Stockholm, 1926).

23. *Ibid.*, 117-18.

24. See, for example, his comments on 3.7-9 (*Ezekiel*, 1.91); 13.2-9 (1.245-46); 17.22-24 (1.324).

25. *Ibid.*, 26.

26. 'Vision of Jerusalem', 148.

27. *Ezekiel*, 1.26-27.

28. See, for example, his comments on Ezek. 12 and 17.17 (*ibid.*, 1.215, 315) and my discussion of Ezek. 17 in Chapter 4 below.

29. 'Vision of Jerusalem', 149.

30. I am inclined to think it is not. John Barton presents a good discussion of the problem in the post-exilic period (*Oracles of God*, 55-75).

31. 'Structuring of Biblical Books', 325.

32. וכל שומע היה משנה; the verb משנה may also be taken as 'study', 'teach', 'repeat'.

33. 'Literary Structuring', 317.

34. *Ibid.*

35. Cf. BT, *Baba Bathra* 15a: אנשי כנסת הגדולה כתבו...יחזקאל ושנים עשר דניאל ומגילת אסתר ('The men of the Great Assembly "wrote"... Ezekiel and [the Book of] the Twelve, Daniel and the Scroll of Esther'). While כתבו may indicate nothing more than production of an official transcription or publication, Rashi notes the theological issue: ואיני יודע למה ('but I לא כתבו יחזקאל בעצמו אם לא מפני שלא נתנה נבואה ליכתב בחוצה לארץ do not know why Ezekiel could not have written it himself unless it is because prophecy may not be written outside the [Holy] Land').

36. *Commentary on the Prophets*, 4.13.

37. *Ibid.*, 4.16.

38. *Ibid.*, 1.64.

39. *Das Buch Ezechiel*, 3.

40. The term is taken from Pratt's discussion of style as a context-dependent phenomenon (*Speech Act Theory*, 81-91 *et passim*).

41. Those (e.g. Bertholet, Fohrer) who propose to find two separate speeches (in second and third persons respectively) which have here been interwoven have failed to produce convincing results.

42. The phrase is from Lindblom, who points to the obvious unlikelihood

of Ezekiel's ever having assembled the corrupt prophets of Israel to hear themselves denounced (*Prophecy in Ancient Israel*, 154).

43. 'Spoken and Written Word', 42.

44. See Talmon's comment, cited above, that the prophet did not bind his teaching upon his students in a single form only. The massive difference between the Hebrew and the Greek texts supports this view.

45. A very useful discussion of the problem of final authorial intentions in modern literatures, including these and other examples, is offered by Jerome J. McGann, *A Critique of Modern Textual Criticism* (Chicago: University of Chicago Press, 1983).

*Notes to Chapter 2*

1. Sumerian proverb from a tablet belonging to the library of Ashurbanipal, cited by Lambert, *Babylonian Wisdom* (Sm. 61, 1.19), 259.

2. BT *Ḥagigah* 13b.

3. To what extent those remaining in Judah were also literarily productive remains an open question. See Enno Janssen, *Juda in der Exilszeit* (Göttingen: Vandenhoeck & Ruprecht, 1956), and Morton Smith, 'Jewish Religious Life in the Persian Period', *Cambridge History of Judaism*, ed. W.D. Davies and Louis Finkelstein (Cambridge: Cambridge University Press, 1984), 1.219-78.

4. *Gamla Testamentet* (Stockholm: Svenska kyrkans diakonistyrelses bokförlag, 1945), 42, quoted in Nielsen, *Oral Tradition*, 33. The notion was earlier articulated by H.S. Nyberg; see Widengren, *Literary and Psychological Aspects*, 8-9.

5. Ackroyd, 'Continuity', 232.

6. George Mendenhall, 'Biblical History in Transition', in *The Bible and the Ancient Near East*, ed. G.E. Wright (Garden City: Doubleday, 1961), 34.

7. The fact that certain paralinguistic indicators are provided by manuscript style or, more markedly, by printing format need not enter into the discussion here, since, in so far as these are features of the biblical text, they are not original.

8. Ricoeur, *Hermeneutics*, 147.

9. 'Context in Written Language: The Case of Imaginative Fiction', in Tannen, *Spoken and Written Language*, 186.

10. *Ibid.*, 187.

11. *Ibid.*, 197.

12. Ricoeur, *Hermeneutics*, 148-49.

13. Concerning the oral poet, A.B. Lord observes: 'Expression is his

business, not originality, which, indeed, is a concept quite foreign to him and one that he would avoid, if he understood it. To say that the *opportunity* for originality and for finding the 'poetically' fine phrase exists does *not* mean that the *desire* for originality also exists. There are periods and styles in which originality is *not* at a premium' (*The Singer of Tales* [Cambridge: Harvard University Press, 1960], 44–45; italics his).

14. A kind of oral performance which differs from the 'bard and formula' style treated by Lord is found among the Athabaskans of Canada and Alaska (see Scollon and Scollon, 'Literacy'). The story is actually interactively produced, with the 'storyteller' providing the background information and organization and individual members of the audience completing each verse with an appropriate word or phrase. The dynamic of 'everyone addressing everyone else', characteristic of all oral transmission of traditional material, is especially evident here, for each stanza must be negotiated and agreement reached before the story can proceed.

15. Olson, 'Utterance', 266.

16. Havelock, *Preface*, 26.

17. *Ibid.*, 47.

18. Ricoeur, *Hermeneutics*, 132-34.

19. *Ibid.*, 142.

20. See Rader in Tannen, *Spoken and Written Language*, 197.

21. The targeting of particular words is crucial here. According to Ong, the cognitive breakthrough associated with writing is effected not by pictographic representations of objects, which are intelligible only with reference to concrete life situations (and thus remain embedded in the oral thought-world), but by the more abstract capability of representing sounds and thereby utterances, the exact words of a real or imagined speaker (see Ong, *Orality*, 83-85).

22. Goody, *Domestication*, 4-5; Goody and Watt, 'Consequences', 48-49.

23. For a refutation of the concept of 'oral literature', see Ong, *Orality*, 10-15.

24. Cf. B. Bernstein, quoted in Hirsch, *Philosophy*, 24.

25. Ong, *Orality*, 26.

26. This notion of rhetoric as a technology should be distinguished from the academic discipline of the same name, which occupied such a prominent place in classical and medieval educational curricula and has recently begun to be revived as an independent field of study. There is some relation between the two: consideration of how deliberately structured language could best be applied to the task of public persuasion in Athenian democracy gave birth to rhetoric as an academic discipline. However, it should not be assumed that rhetorical practice or theory developed along similar lines or occupied a comparable place in ancient Near Eastern cultures.

27. It is retrospectively accurate to make use of the term 'transitional' in

order to indicate rhetoric's historical situation between the stages of primarily oral composition and transmission of material and widespread reliance upon writing. It should not, however, be inferred that there is anything inherently defective, unstable, or exceptional about this mode which orients itself in significant ways toward both writing and speaking. Finnegan's observation is apt: 'On the contrary the kind of situation in which there is *some* literacy and written literatures but at the same time an absence of mass literacy, accompanied not surprisingly by circulation of literature in oral form, often with at least some interaction of written literature—this situation is probably much more common throughout the world today and perhaps also throughout many centuries of human history, than that of the purely oral setting' ('How Oral?', 57; italics hers).

28. Goody, *Domestication*, 116.

29. It is regrettable that little direct help is so far available from those outside the biblical field. Discussion of the emergence of literacy as a major cultural force has, under Havelock's influence, focused on Athens in the middle of the first millenium, where widespread use of a fully vocalized alphabet is held to be the great watershed in the history of writing. Havelock asserts that the difficulty of deciphering the 'syllabic' West Semitic writing system was so great as to require professional management, and that writing was therefore confined to a professional scribal class whose job it was to make 'a series of decisions basically acoustic in nature' (*Prologue*, 7). The classification of West Semitic writing as a syllabary is insupportable (see, for example, Barr, 'Reading', and Cross, 'Origin', 11) and the conclusion about the extent of Israelite literacy is consequently dubious, although the evidence is not wholly clear (see discussion below, pp. 42f.). Havelock's inference that the nature of the script is determinative of its cultural impact and, finally, the complexity of what it can express is simplistic.

30. Demsky comments: 'In essence the prophetic presentation or act is a striking example of *the bridging process between a literate group and a lay audience*' (*Biblical Archaeology Today*, 351; italics his).

31. 'Rôle', 40-41. Widengren expresses a similar view: 'The process of recording, collecting, and preserving the master's words and actions, both in Israelite and Muslim religious literature, is from the outset bound up with the process of committing the traditions to paper. . . . But learnt by heart, read aloud and dictated, *the texts were nevertheless always written and this was their manner of transmission* (*Literary and Psychological Aspects*, 88, 91; italics his).

32. On the basis of the prophets' use of images, metaphors, and realistic references which show familiarity with writing, Demsky observes: 'One must deduce that the world of the prophet and his listeners was steeped in the consciousness of writing' ('Literacy', 138).

33. *Wisdom*, 17.

34. Lang observes: 'But the high level of Israel's writing seems to me scarcely comprehensible completely without formal school instruction' ('Schule', 192); see his discussion of prophetic education (*Monotheism*, 96-100). Crenshaw posits the existence of various guilds for priests, prophets, potters, musicians, *et al*. ('Education', 614n).

35. Demsky cites Ezek. 33.30ff. in this regard ('Education', 397), although it is doubtful that the simile lends itself to such historical inference; Lemaire finds (late) evidence of musical training in 1 Chron. 16.4-7; 25.1ff. (*Écoles*, 69). Wiseman suggests that in local sanctuaries, prophets taught writing and rhetoric to young male students ('Books', 38).

36. On Ezekiel's Zadokite affiliation, see Wilson, *Prophecy and Society*, 282.

37. Eichrodt, *Ezekiel*, 22.

38. *Orality*, 119, 132.

39. These characteristics are, of course, even more true of scrolls than of codices, which do not seem to have come into common usage until the first century CE, and then only within Christian communities. See C.H. Roberts and T.C. Skeat, *The Birth of the Codex* (London/New York: Oxford University Press, 1983).

40. The fears expressed by Plato (in the *Phaedrus* and the *Seventh Letter*) about writing replacing the exercise of memory have been realized only in modern print cultures. The relation between writing and memorization in rabbinic culture has been treated by B. Gerhardsson, *Memory and Manuscript* (Uppsala: Almqvist & Wiksells; Lund: C.W.K. Gleerup, 1961) and by M. Jousse (*Manducation*, see pp. 52f. below), and in medieval culture by F. Yates, *The Art of Memory* (Chicago: University of Chicago, 1966). The Hebrew word קְרָא ('read', literally 'call aloud') attests to the persistence of oral habits in reading from manuscripts, a phenomenon which is disguised in the standard translation of מִקְרָא as 'Scripture'.

41. Burrows describes the prophet's style as 'a veritable tissue of remembrances' and comments: 'His mind was saturated with the ideas and the language of the writers who preceded him, and when he wrote he reproduced thoughts and expressions as they came to him. He did not look up his quotations or verify his references; he simply read, marked, pondered, and inwardly digested, then spoke out of a full mind. . .' (*Literary Relations*, 14). The observation is apt, despite the fact that Burrows considers this prophet to have been an *ex tempore* orator of pre-Maccabean times.

42. B. Porten suggests three periods when Israelites and Judaeans might have settled in Egypt; the last 35 years of the eighth century, from the Syro-Ephraimite War to the Assyrian siege of Jerusalem; the mid-eighth century, when Manasseh brought troops to fight with Psammetichus I against the Assyrians; and the period between Jehoiakim's accession (609) and the

assassination of Gedaliah (582?) (*Archives from Elephantine* [Berkeley: University of California Press, 1968], 8-16).

43. *Domestication*, 15.

44. Laessøe, 'Literacy', 216.

45. See Widengren, *Literary and Psychological Aspects*, 61.

46. Demsky, 'Literacy', 117-32; Naveh, 'Paleographic Note', 68-71. A recent summary of Demsky's argument is available in English in *Biblical Archaeology Today*, 351-53; a fuller work, *Literacy in Ancient Israel* (Jerusalem: Bialik Institute), is forthcoming. Ben Zion Dinor also infers from the biblical evidence that in the pre-exilic period, reading and writing were ordinary capabilities, learned and practiced in the home (e.g. at holiday recitations of the ancestral traditions) as well as in public affairs ('Education', 118-19).

47. Although inscriptional evidence from the mid-eighth century to the exile is especially plentiful, it is debatable whether this is due wholly to an increase in writing, over against the early monarchic period, or whether it reflects in part the fact that periods of violent destruction and sudden abandonment of sites generally yield more archaeological data than those of long peaceful settlement.

48. Millard, *Biblical Archaeology Today*, 307; cf. also Demsky, 'Writing', 655.

49. See Demsky, *Biblical Archaeology Today*, 350.

50. 'Literacy', 26.

51. Scollon and Scollon offer their typology in order to suggest rather than exhaust the varieties of literacy. With respect to ancient Israel, further distinctions within the pragmatic category should certainly be made. For example, the ability to decipher or even write personal names or common words (as in labels or lists) requires a much lower level of skill than does reading, let alone composing, sentences in letters and other documents. Probably many people who were able to do the former still resorted to a scribe on the rare occasions when they had need for the latter.

52. *Yoma* I.6: אם רגיל לקרות קורא, ואם לאו קורין לפניו ('If he is accustomed to read, he shall read; and if not, they shall read in his presence').

53. *On Literacy*, 54.

54. 'Citations', 275.

55. Harry Orlinsky argues that the biblical expression for 'designating a document as official and binding, in other words, as divinely inspired, as Sacred Scripture' is קרא באזני העם, 'read in the ears of the people' ('The Septuagint as Holy Writ and the Philosophy of the Translators', *HUCA* 46 [1975], 94).

56. Oliver observes that, whereas the Greeks seem to have used writing first to preserve oral poetry, it may well have been the case in ancient India

that works originally composed in writing were preserved by oral transmission ('Some Aspects', 58).

57.   See Gitay's comments on the stylistic and functional similarities of speech and early writing ('Deutero-Isaiah', 189-94).

## Notes to Chapter 3

1.   This suggestion has recently been reiterated and further specified by Vogt ('Lähmung und Stummheit').

2.   *Ezekiel*, 1.121.

3.   That 3.16b-21 interrupts an original unity between 3.16a and 3.22 is agreed by Herrmann, Cooke, Fohrer, Zimmerli, Wilson, et al. While Greenberg's denial of such a disturbance (*Ezekiel*, 1.81-82) is consistent with his general desire to maintain the integrity of the received text, in this instance it seems to run counter to his own argument for seeing the restriction of movement and speech as directly consequent upon Ezekiel's seven-day desolation.

4.   'Interpretation of Ezekiel's Dumbness', 101.

5.   Note the repetition of כל ('all') in 36.2-4.

6.   *Ezekiel*, 1.68.

7.   *Manducation*, 45-53.

8.   Another vivid physical image of the connections among orality, writing, and learning may be seen in the Hellenistic practice of ingesting magical inscriptions in order to facilitate their memorization (see Bror Olsson, 'Die verschlungene Buchrolle', *ZNW* 32 [1933], 90-91).

9.   Note Greenberg's interpretation of דבר ב־, cited above.

10.   See pp. 58f. below.

11.   Ong, *Presence*, 22-35; *Orality*, 57-68.

12.   Cf. p. 23 above.

13.   *Prophets*, 4.42.

14.   The work of Greenberg, Talmon and Fishbane is especially helpful in demonstrating recurrent habits or 'principles' of Ezekiel's composition.

15.   *Contra* Ewald's judgment that the expression in 3.25 is so definite that it must refer to some particular incident.

16.   Zimmerli, on the other hand, adopts this solution in his translation, but without clear defense (*Ezekiel*, 1.147-48).

17.   *Ezekiel*, 1.102.

18.   For this translation, see Moshe Greenberg, 'The Hebrew Oath Particle ḤAY/ḤÊ', *JBL* 76 (1957), 34-39.

19.   That the shift has hardly been noted by most scholars is perhaps due to the fact that the interactive nature of prophecy has itself not been sufficiently treated, although Gunkel observed that much prophetic speech is incompre-

hensible unless viewed as having occurred in the context of dialogue. The role of feedback in the prophetic process is discussed by Thomas Overholt, 'Jeremiah and the Nature of the Prophetic Process', in *Scripture in History and Theology*, ed. A.L. Merrill and T.W. Overholt (Allison Park, PA: Pickwick Press, 1977), 129-50.

20. The inference here is only that there is conscious continuity between the two prophetic traditions and not that the scroll which Ezekiel eats is specifically intended to be understood as Jeremiah's. Eichrodt comments on 2.8-10: 'It points to the preaching of the prophets, already at that time frequently recorded in writing, the most influential example of which is the collected words of Jeremiah dictated to Baruch' (*Ezekiel*, 62); cf. Zimmerli, *Ezekiel*, 1.137.

21. A stylistic singularity occurs here to highlight the arrival of the refugee and the lifting of the dumbness as the pivot point of the book. In 31.21-22, Ezekiel departs from his convention elsewhere by moving into first-person narration without reference to a divine speech or vision.

22. Greenberg's rendering of the phrase פּתחון פֹה, literally 'opening of the mouth' (of the redeemed Israel, 16.63, and of Ezekiel, 29.21), as 'a claim to be heard'—based on its Mishnaic meanings, 'an occasion for complaint, a pretext for accusation'—supports this interpretation (*Ezekiel*, 1.121).

23. So Zimmerli, *Ezekiel*, 2.185.

24. It is significant, in view of what was said above (pp. 48ff.) about prophecy ceasing to be a two-directional form of communication, that neither of these acts of 'intercession' occurs at the people's request.

25. 'King Joiachin', 54.

26. With respect to Claude Lévi-Strauss's demonstration of the complexity of historical dating systems as involving many discontinuous subsets (*The Savage Mind* [Chicago: University of Chicago Press, 1966], 258-62), Goody comments: 'The whole process he describes is a fine example of the kind of formalisation that is encouraged by visuo-spatial communication, and particularly by the setting down of language in written form' (*Domestication*, 149).

27. That such a dating system was recognized as a mark of authenticity in prophetic speech is indicated by its imitation in Haggai and Zechariah.

28. *Ezekiel*, 1.113.

29. The work of Malamat ('Twilight of Judah') is especially valuable. See also Greenberg's useful table and summary of the evidence, *Ezekiel*, 1.8-11.

30. דרש את־יי is a technical term designating a request for a prophetic audience in which the petitioner seeks to know the outcome of a particular course of events in either the personal or the political sphere (cf. 1 Kgs 14.5, 22.8; 2 Kgs 8.8; 22.13; Jer. 21.2; 37.7).

31. See JPS's translation of אני יי נענה-לו בי, 14.7, 'I the LORD will

respond to him directly'. Zimmerli's explanation of the unusual niphal—'an arbitrariness in the language of Ezekiel which seeks to give expression to the almost passive "to allow oneself to be forced to answer"' (*Ezekiel*, 1.301)— misses the point that the change here is not toward passivity on God's part but to unilateral control of the revelatory process. Far from being arbitrary, the verb form is a precise departure from the conventional which underscores the contrast between the presently decreed conditions for prophecy and the popular expectation (expressed in לדרש־לו בי, 'in order to make inquiry through him of me').

32. 'Dates in Ezekiel', 470. I do not accept their judgment that the passage ends with vv. 30-31 (see the detailed discussion of this passage in Chapter 5 below).

33. Freedy and Redford associate the elders' inquiry in ch. 20 with Psammetichus II's tour of Palestine, which they date to 591, and speculate that their question was whether this show of Egyptian strength did not indicate the coming defeat of Nebuchadnezzar. Malamat's argument that the date of the tour should be corrected to 592 is convincing, and his further suggestion that the event lying behind this inquiry is expiration of the two-year period set by Hananiah (cf. Jer. 27–28) is highly attractive. But the correction does not affect the validity of Freedy and Redford's point cited here.

34. Appreciation of the imaginative or metaphorical character of the discourse is pertinent to setting guidelines for evaluation of the text's history. On these grounds, for example, one may challenge Eichrodt's claim tht the references to child sacrifice and idolatry in ch. 20 are illogical and unhistorical intrusions of the Deuteronomic redactors *Ezekiel*, 274-76), since the truth and logic of poetic (understood in a broad sense) works must be judged differently from those of expository prose.

35. 'Parallels', 150.

36. Regarding the conjectured dates, see Greenberg, *Ezekiel*, 1.10.

37. *Kein Aufstand*, 158-59.

38. M. Weber, *Das antike Judentum* (Tübingen: J.C.B. Mohr, 1921), 285; quoted in Lang, *Monotheism*, 81.

39. כסף in 22.18 is problematic. BHS suggests omission or transposition to the head of the list of metals (cf. v. 20); S.R. Driver (*A Treatise on the Use of the Tenses in Hebrew* [Oxford: Clarendon Press, 1892], 249) reads the two words as appositional, the second qualifying the first: 'silver dross'; G.R. Driver ('Linguistic and Textual Problems: Ezekiel,' *Biblica* 19 [1938], 69) emends to סיג מכסף, 'dross without silver'; Zimmerli omits it. It is very difficult to read (with JPS) 'the dross shall turn into silver', which is contradictory both to experience and to what follows.

40. Zimmerli dates vv. 23-31 after 587, because the final judgment has taken place. The 'converted imperfect' verbs in v. 31 allow such an

interpretation, but they may also be taken as expressing certitude.

41. Ezra and ben Sirach are the only pre-rabbinic scholars he recognizes (*Monotheism*, 140).

42. *Ibid.*, 155-56.

43. Carley, *Ezekiel among the Prophets*, 157.

44. 'Israelite Prophecy', 52-53.

45. Freedman, 'Book of Ezekiel', 453.

46. Greenberg, 'Ezekiel' (*Enc. Jud.*), 108.

47. See John Skinner, *Prophecy and Religion: Studies in the Life of Jeremiah* (Cambridge; Cambridge University Press, 1922), 201; and von Rad's argument to the contrary, 'Die Confessionen Jeremias', *Evangelische Theologie* 3 (1936), 265-76.

48. Freedman, 'Book of Ezekiel', 453.

49. BT *Sanhedrin*, 39a.

50. *Guide for the Perplexed*, II, 46.

51. *Symbolische Handlungen*, 91.

52. *Kein Aufstand*, 168.

53. 'Special Form- and Traditio-Historical Character', 520.

54. Several times (12.9; 24.19; 37.18) a supposed popular request for clarification provides the occasion for (divine) explication of the sign-action.

55. *Ezechiel*, 3-4.

56. *Interfaces of the Word*, 72.

57. *Ezekiel*, 1.183.

58. Because of the time and travel involved, Jer. 13.1-7, like several of Ezekiel's sign-actions, has little communicative value as an actual performance. It, too, must be regarded as a literary figure.

59. Gunkel, for example, contrasts Jeremiah's deep suffering with Ezekiel's lack of sympathy, cruelty, and bitterness born of strife ('Die Propheten als Schriftsteller', lxx).

60. 'Israelite Prophecy', 53.

*Notes to Chapter 4*

1. *Rhetoric of Fiction*, 396-97.

2. Iser, 'Indeterminacy', 14.

3. 'Narrative Analysis', 37.

4. Verse 3, which is wholly unique in its reference to the prophet in the third person, appears to be an addition from another editorial hand.

5. Predictably, some have suggested alternate readings: the thirteenth year (Bertholet), בשלם שנה (Tur-Sinai, although the posited equivalence to תם שנ[ה] in Lev. 25.29 is by no means clear). There is no manuscript or versional support for an emendation.

6. Spiegel, 'Ezekiel', 290.

7. The situation of the modern reader with respect to the phrase is, of course, very different from that of Ezekiel's contemporaries. I assume that the frame of reference for 'the thirtieth year' was at one time known, either to few or to many. But now, because the phrase cannot finally be decoded, there is really no possibility of forming an in-group of those who understand. If, then, we are not all to be excluded from the text on this basis, it is necessary that the phrase be rendered inoperative: instead of a rhetorical device, it becomes a scholarly crux.

8. The suggestion that this may refer to a martyrs' cult was made by Robert Wilson (private communication).

9. *Ezekiel*, 1.492.

10. Hammershaimb points to the idea of a remnant, in the sense of a small group who *on account of their righteousness* escape the fate of the guilty majority, as a new interpretation of the remnant idea (previously associated purely with God's mercy and not with human deserving) produced in the exilic period (*Some Aspects of Old Testament Prophecy*, 110).

11. It is interesting, although not directly related to the conditions surrounding the original production of the book, that rabbinic tradition seems repeatedly to have restricted the public reading and even private study of Ezekiel. Chapter 1 was for some time banned as a *haftarah* reading in the liturgy (*Mishnah Megillah* 4.10, cf. *Tosefta Megillah* 4.34); a minimum age limit of thirty was set for its study (BT *Ḥagigah* 13b), and restrictions were imposed even on the class size (*Mishnah Ḥagigah* 2.1). John Barton suggests that the rabbinic discussion concerning the 'withdrawal' (גנז) of Ezekiel (BT *Shabbat* 13b; *Ḥagigah* 13a; *Menaḥot* 45a) entails, not its scriptural status, but specifically the question of liturgical use: 'I do think it likely in any case that the issue of "withdrawal" has to do with the belief that inconsistencies in Scripture are a danger to the simple, not because they show Scripture to be imperfect (God forbid!) but *because they are a signal that the text contains deeper meanings which are best left to the learned*' (*Oracles of God*, 72; italics his). This means, then, that at least portions of the book were considered (by the rabbis if not the prophet himself) to be suited only to an in-group. the point is reinforced by stories of the child who 'apprehended what *ḥashmal* was, whereupon a fire went forth from *ḥashmal* and consumed him' (BT *Ḥagigah* 13a), or again, of four sages who entered the mystical *pardes*, but only one (Akiba) returned in safety (*Ḥagigah* 14b).

12. The relationship is underscored in God's speech by the frequent references to 'your [Ezekiel's] people' after the fall. עמך occurs in 26.11; 33.2, 12, 17, 30; 37.18; the only occurrences in the pre-fall section are in bound phrases: בני עמך (3.11, here referring specifically to the exiles) and בנות עמך (13.17, in reference to the false prophetesses).

13. Wayne Booth observes: 'But the very effectiveness of the rhetoric

designed to produce sympathy might in itself lead to a serious misreading of the book. In reducing the emotional distance, the natural tendency is to reduce—willy-nilly—moral and intellectual distance as well' (*Rhetoric*, 249).

14. *Ezekiel*, 2.201.

15. Even more overt reference to Vergil's authorial identity and earlier accomplishments is found in the opening words excised by his ancient literary executors:

> Ille ego, qui quondam gracili modulatus avena
> carmen, et egressus silvis vicina coegi
> ut quamvis avido parerent arva colono
> gratum opus agricolis; at nunc horrentia Martis
> *arma virumque cano*. . .

('I am he, who once tuned a song by a slender shepherd's pipe, and then, having left the woods, compelled the neighboring fields to yield to the tiller—however greedy—a work pleasing to farmers; but now *of Mars' bristling implements and of men I sing*. . .').

16. It is interesting that Greene cites the 'architectonic quality'—the same word frequently applied to Ezekiel's prophecy—of the Homeric poems as an indication that they were composed by a literary process, using notes or outlines ('Spoken and Written Word', 29). The idea that the *Iliad* is a textual creation is assumed by James Boyd White, who argues skillfully that Homer uses the inherited language of oral epic in an ironic fashion, i.e., to criticize that cultural world and its values (*When Words Lose their Meaning*, [Chicago: University of Chicago Press, 1984], 24-58).

17. Once (24.21-24) only does Ezekiel seem to betray his own hand inadvertently, gliding from divine speech (v. 21) to the prophetic 'I' (v. 22) and back to divine speech referring to himself in the third person (v. 24).

18. As indicated above, the problem is not one of open hostility but of willful incomprehension and failure to take seriously Ezekiel's message of doom, as long as more attractive prophetic alternatives are available.

19. *Literary and Psychological Aspects*, 118.

20. *Ibid.*, 117.

21. *Ezekiel*, 1.36.

22. 'Citations', 278.

23. An interesting comparison to Ezekiel's adept narrative manipulation is afforded by the book of Haggai, which shows Ezekiel's influence in its dating frame and also contains what seems to be a failed attempt to adopt his theocentric perspective. Interrogation of the priests in 2.10-15, at first incorporated within an oracle, almost unnoticeably (v. 12b) becomes a direct report of dialogue.

24. *Nature of Narrative*, 241.

25. The terms are Zimmerli's; see his discussion, *Ezekiel*, 1.36. Adoption

of his designation here, however, does not signify acceptance of each of these passages as an independent oracle (see the discussion of 20.32-44 in Chapter 5 below).

26. Ong observes that the rhetorical tradition (which, as discussed in Chapter 2 above, arose as a writing-dependent phenomenon in cultures still oriented largely to oral communication) 'helped in the fictionalizing of the audience of learned works in a generic but quite real way. Rhetoric fixed knowledge in agonistic structures' (*Interfaces*, 76). Concerning the further development of the disputation form in biblical literature, Zimmerli notes that in the book of Malachi 'we can see the beginning of the true doctrinal disputation which became of great importance in Talmudic Judaism' (*Ezekiel*, 1.280).

27. Fontaine, *Traditional Sayings*, 150.

28. *Ibid.*, 152.

29. Here the citation is from Chinua Achebe's novel, *Things Fall Apart* (London: Heinemann, 1958), 92; cf. Seitel's discussion, 'Proverbs', 135-36.

30. Greenberg suggests that the phrase עלה על/מעלות רוח (11.5, with reference to 11.3; 20.32) indicates that the formulation of the popular attitude is Ezekiel's own and not something he actually heard ('Citations', 274).

31. The opposite sense has sometimes been inferred, but it involves some contrivance. Eichrodt emends (in accordance with the LXX) to read: 'Have not the houses lately been rebuilt?' Rashi splits the reference and paraphrases: 'The doom predicted by the prophets is not close [cf. 12.22], so let us build houses and settle in them!'

32. See pp. 61f. above.

33. 'Biblical Hermeneutics', 78-79.

34. Wheelwright offers a perceptive discussion of the ways in which metaphors may be enriched by repeated usage, thereby expanding their fields of association and reference (*Metaphor and Reality*, 92-110). In his terminology, this constitutes a progression from metaphor to symbol, which may function, among other possibilities, at a personal level (within the corpus of a single poet's work, or even within one piece, e.g. 'metamorphosis' for Ovid), as 'symbols of ancestral vitality' (referring to older written sources; T.S. Eliot's *The Waste Land* is an outstanding—some might say, aggravated—example of such allusive technique), or as 'symbols of cultural range' (meaningful in terms of the understandings and practice of a particular social group).

35. Consider, for example, the vine as an image of God's particular establishment and tending of Israel in Ps. 80.15-16, and its perversion to an image of apostasy in Isa. 5.1-7.

36. It is not clear here whether 17.8 represents the vine's inappropriate aspiration for growth under the second eagle or a statement of its condition under the first eagle, thereby reinforcing the illogic of the defection.

37. That this is the meaning of the unusual plural (rather than 'among the interwoven foliage' [<עבת; cf. Brown–Driver–Briggs–Gesenius, 721b]), seems certain from its application to the cedar. To say that its top was among other trees would dwarf its magnificence.

38. There is no need to adopt the common emendation of אשור (31.3) to תאשור ('box-tree'), whose stature would hardly be likely to excite arboreal envy (31.9); furthermore, all the ancient versions support the reading אשור. Moshe Greenberg (in an oral communication) points out that the question posed here to Egypt, 'Whom do you resemble?', to which the answer is 'Assyria', complements Nahum's question to Assyria, 'Are you better than No Amon [Egyptian Thebes, which Assyrian had previously destroyed]?' (3.8). In both cases, the rhetorical task is to show the inevitable downfall of a seemingly impregnable power, and the prophet's strategy is to invite a comparison between the ruling giant and one which has already toppled.

39. The term is von Rabenau's ('Die Form des Rätsels', 129); cf. p. 63 above.

40. The astute medieval commentator, Eliezer of Beaugency, considered this unusual heading as indicating something about the rhetorical effect of the passage: 'Perhaps the words will enter into their hearts, and they will tell their brethren who are in the land, and they will repent' (*ad loc.*).

41. See James Crenshaw's discussion of the חירה in *Old Testament Form Criticism*, ed. John H. Hayes (San Antonio: Trinity University Press, 1974), 240-41.

42. *Ezekiel*, 1.360.

43. Recent examples of this latter approach are offered by Eichrodt and Wevers. The solution which Zimmerli adopts, that the interpretation is altogether a *post eventum* addition, was first proposed in 1836 by Jan van Gilse (*Specimen exegeticum et criticum exhibens commentarium in c. XVII vaticinorum Ezechielis* [Amsterdam]). His judgment was based upon discrepancies between allegory and interpretation, such as the mention of oath and covenant in the latter alone. While Zimmerli remains agnostic on the question of authorship, Garscha and Hossfeld follow Hölscher in denying any part of the interpretation of Ezekiel and finding evidence of several strata within the material, although they develop their arguments on different premises (Hossfeld seems to attribute vv. 1-10 to the prophet, whereas Garscha thinks that one can only trace the bare outline of a vine image originally belonging to prophetic speech).

44. Lang, *Kein Aufstand*, 28-88; Greenberg, *Ezekiel*, 1.309-24. Polk's study ('Paradigms, Parables', 578-83) also considers the means by which this chapter as a whole achieves its rhetorical effect, although he does not raise the questions of its compositional history.

45. *Kein Aufstand*, 48.

46. Greenberg agrees with Lang that the riddle is, in the first interpretation

section (vv. 12b-18), correctly solved by supplying political referents for the figures, although he shows also how one could devise a nearly satisfactory solution by reading the fable as a coded account of apostasy: the great eagle is YHWH; the lesser one, a foreign deity; the cedar, Israel; etc. Accordingly, Greenberg sees the effect of the first interpretation section to lie largely in the surprise that 'for once the prophet had gotten off his theocentric hobbyhorse and had dealt with human events!' (*Ezekiel* 1.321). He then posits a 'planar leap' to the second interpretation (vv. 19-21), wherein 'the political transaction is used as a model from which a theological analogy is drawn' (*ibid.*, 1.322).

47. *Kein Aufstand*, 33.

48. BHS proposes כנצר or כשמר instead of כנשר, but without versional or manuscript evidence. More plausible, however, is Tur-Sinai's suggestion that the word intended is cognate with Arabic *naššār*, 'herald' (James Barr, *Comparative Philology and the Text of the Old Testament* [Winona Lake, IN: Eisenbrauns, 1987], 26f.

49. Cf. Ezek. 16.29; other prophets also play on the original sense of 'Canaan' in reference to merchant trade (specifically, Phoenician purple trade): Hos. 12.8; Zeph. 1.11; Zech. 14.21.

50. Cf. Jeremiah's concept of Nebuchadnezzar as 'servant of YHWH' (25.9; 27.6; 43.10).

51. *Kein Aufstand*, 33.

52. *Ibid.*, 1.365.

53. *Ezekiel*, 1.321

54. Equally unacceptable is Zimmerli's streamlining of the text, which involves dismissal of the East Wind as deviating from 'the original plan of the fable', in which an eagle-avenger alone was presumably portrayed (*Ezekiel*, 1.363).

55. Without attempting to level literary history, one may note that the combination of fable and interpretation bears some resemblance to the exegetical pattern familiar from rabbinic literature, that of *mashal* and *nimshal*. The rabbis explicate the biblical verse, first through an analogy cast in the form of a metaphorical narrative, and then through a non-figurative (or perhaps, according to modern sensibilities, less figurative) discourse relating the narrative both to the verse at hand and, in a larger sense, to the interaction between God and Israel in history. The important point is that *mashal* and *nimshal* together form a rhetorical unit, whose joint purpose is not only to illumine a scriptural text, but also to produce a reading which reflects the present concerns of the rabbis and their audience. This rhetorical intention, then, performs a unifying function and, further, connects the narrative, in both its figurative and descriptive aspects, to the world. The *mashal* is an open system, equally informed by and commenting on Scripture and extra-textual reality (see the discussion by David Stern, 'Rhetoric and

Midrash', 276). Although there is no warrant for seeing the rabbis' *mashal* as patterned on Ezekiel's, the rabbinic model is nonetheless useful in demonstrating how figure and interpretation may cooperate in serving a single rhetorical end.

56. Such an assumption seems to underlie Zimmerli's analysis. He treats glimpses of political reality within the metaphorical section (e.g., 'city of traders', v. 4; 'many people', v. 9) as unintentional intrusions influenced by the interpretation.

57. The vagueness of the term את־ עשה is further demonstrated by the fact that Ezekiel uses it in both positive and negative senses (7.27; 20.44; note that את־ is in the first case pointed as the accusative particle, in the second as a preposition).

58. The weakness of the synchronic position on this verse is further indicated by the strained arguments brought to bear on the surrounding verses. Greenberg's assertion that the reference to Zedekiah's fate in v. 16 would be far more detailed and horrifying had the events attending his deportation already occurred (*Ezekiel*, 1.323-24) is particularly unconvincing. Literary creation involves many more factors than the amount of information available at the time of composition; rhetorical purpose, interaction between a given passage and others within the work or the tradition, aesthetic considerations, etc., also play a part. It is illegitimate to speculate on the limits of a writer's knowledge based solely on what is omitted from the text (cf. Greenberg's own observation regarding chs. 40–48 that 'omissions cannot serve as a warrant for negative conclusions' ['Design and Themes', 193]). Lang argues that the attempt to differentiate the image chronologically from what follows represents a misunderstanding of Ezekiel's intention, which is not to discover in the past the roots of the political catastrophe, but rather to prevent its actual occurrence in the present (*Kein Aufstand*, 54). In the present passage, however, it is difficult to reconcile that hope of averting disaster with the firm assertions in vv. 16 and 18 that the Judean king will not escape death in Babylon.

59. There is, of course, no proof that it was Ezekiel who provided the correction. However, since the error became evident within his period of activity, I see no reason to suppose another hand.

60. So Eichrodt argues on the basis of 'the prose form which makes it conspicuously different from its surroundings' (*Ezekiel*, 226). Other formal considerations seem to me more persuasive evidence that these three verses can be treated as an inserted unit. If they are removed, the rhetorical force of v. 19 with its powerful threefold introduction—לכן כה־אמר אדני יי חי־אני ('Therefore thus says YHWH, by my life')—is much enhanced as an answer to the rhetorical question in v. 15. Moreover, that answer is then rendered first of all in the theological terms characteristic of Ezekiel's prophecy: God emerges directly as the offended party and the avenger of bad faith. While

the triple repetition of the phrase 'despise oath ... break covenant' only occurs in the final form of the text, another related pattern (and, indeed, a sharper progression) emerges in what may once have been successive verses: בריתו ('his covenant', v. 14), ברית ('covenant', v. 15), בריתי ('my covenant', v. 19). Verses 16-18 also show coherence in their content: an assertion and reassertion of the cause and ineluctability of Zedekiah's fate form a ring around a brief account of the lost hope that it could be averted.

61. Zimmerli suggests that the absence of a revelation formula at the head of ch. 19 may indicate that at an earlier editorial stage, ch. 19 was joined directly with ch. 17 (*Ezekiel*, 1.391).

62. The obvious candidates are Judah's exiled kings: Jehoahaz, Jehoiakin, and Zedekiah. The identity of the first cub as Jehoahaz might appear to be secured by the reference to Egypt (19.4). Nonetheless, it is doubtful whether a three-month reign would have been sufficient to earn him a reputation for slaughter (v. 3). The second cub is still more troublesome. On the one hand, if Jehoiakin is intended, the same problem with the brevity of his reign obtains. Some scholars prefer to identify it with the historically more important Zedekiah; the fact that he and Jehoahaz were sons of one mother, Hamutal (2 Kgs 23.31; 24.18) would also seem to fit the allegory. Yet the lion figure suggests that the capture and removal affects only the royal household; the destruction of the nation which came at the time of Zedekiah's exile is better seen in the vine image (vv. 10-14) which is joined, probably editorially, to it. In fact, we cannot name two (let alone two successive) kings who both bore responsibility for depredations of the nation and went into exile.

63. Lang argues (with some justice) against the rigid schematization of the salvation and doom oracles as being pre- and post-fall respectively, but Greenberg acknowledges that the restoration coda here is less necessary to the judgment prophecy than in ch. 16. If Zimmerli is correct in positing an earlier connection between chs. 17 and 19 (cf. note 61 above), then it is likely that 17.22-24 was added after their separation; it is hardly appropriate for the lament to follow the restoration promise without further introduction.

### Notes to Chapter 5

1. 'Die Propheten als Schriftsteller', lxix.
2. *Religion of Israel*, 432.
3. S.R. Driver, *Introduction to the Literature of the Old Testament* (New York: Charles Scribner's Sons, 1913), 279.
4. 'Prolegomenon', xxiii. The latter transference has been more troublesome to modern commentators; this is what prompted Torrey's thesis that the book was originally an historical fiction set in the days of Manasseh.

5.   Robert Scholes offers a similar definition: 'Narrative is a sequencing of something for somebody' ('Language, Narrative, and Anti-Narrative', *On Narrative*, ed. W.J.T. Mitchell, 205). The significance of my alterations should be clear from the discussion to follow.

6.   Pratt, in fact, does go on to categorize natural and literary narratives together in the class of speech acts known as 'representatives' (*Speech Act Theory*, 143).

7.   *Ibid.*, 140

8.   Ricoeur, *Hermeneutics*, 295. Hayden White makes a similar point about the fictional character of historical narratives: 'This value attached to narrativity in the representation of real events arises out of a desire to have real events display the coherence, integrity, fullness, and closure of an image of life that is and can only be imaginary' ('The Value of Narrativity in the Representation of Reality', *On Narrative*, ed. W.J.T. Mitchell, 23). Ricoeur, however, argues convincingly against White that neither is consonance wholly on the side of narrative nor dissonance on that of real experience. Stories incorporate upsetting, unreconciled elements; on the other hand, it is our ordinary habit of ordering experience sequentially and symbolically which makes narrative possible in the first place (*Time and Narrative*, 1.72-74).

9.   *Philosophy and Historical Understanding* (New York: Schocken Books, 1964).

10.   Ricoeur, *Hermeneutics*, 277; cf. *Time and Narrative*, 1.150.

11.   Greenberg, 'Prolegomenon', xxvii.

12.   *Ibid.*, xxv-xxviii.

13.   Such a reinterpretation of the past in light of the present crisis is, of course, the aim of the other great narrative creations of the exilic period: the Deuteronomistic History, the Priestly Work, and, in a more limited sense, the prose sections of Jeremiah. Siegfried Herrmann comments on the connection among the exilic prophets in this regard ('Overcoming the Israelite Crisis', *A Prophet to the Nations*, ed. L.G. Perdue and B.W. Kovacs [Winona Lake: Eisenbrauns, 1984], 306).

14.   *Ezekiel*, 1.412.

15.   *Ibid.*, 1.418.

16.   Greenberg, *Ezekiel*, 1.382-83.

17.   *Ezekiel*, 1.411. Zimmerli shows a better appreciation of the verse's irremediable hardness in another brief discussion ('Message', 145-46).

18.   Eichrodt, *Ezekiel*, 270; Greenberg, *Ezekiel*, 1.369; Zimmerli, *Ezekiel*, 1.411.

19.   *When Prophecy Failed*, 199.

20.   It was, however, not in the wilderness period treated in the present narrative but under the foreign influence and political pressures of the Assyrian era (2 Kgs 16.3; 21.6) that child sacrifice seems to have come into

practice in Israel; the polemics of Jeremiah (32.35) and the Deuteronomist (Deut. 12.29-31) indicate that it continued into the sixth century.

21. Note the alternation of verbs (ידע and זכר) in 16.61-63 and 20.42-44.

22. Rendtorff treats the relation between the two passages in 'Ez 20 und 36,16ff im Rahmen der Komposition des Buches Ezechiel', *Ezekiel and His Book*, ed. J. Lust, 260-65.

23. *Religion of Israel*, 75; cf. Greenberg, *Ezekiel*, 1.190.

24. The centrality of God's act of forgiveness in creating the conditions for obedience is made explicit in the related passage in Jeremiah about the new covenant written on Israel's heart (31.34).

25. See Paul Joyce, *Divine Initiative and Human Response in Ezekiel* (JSOT Supplement Series 50; Sheffield: JSOT Press, 1989).

26. It is significant that in each instance where there appears a general plea for repentance, the context carefully circumscribes the offer. Twice this is achieved through a discussion drawn along the lines of case law, emphasizing the full responsibility for sin and continually renewed opportunity for righteousness which belongs to each generation (18.1-20; cf. Deut. 24.16) and even, in Ezekiel's radical formulation, to each Israelite (18.21-32; 33.10-20); once by the similarly patterned oracle of the three just men (14.12-23, slightly separated from the plea in v. 6), who could save no one but themselves.

27. The fact that many critics deny these chapters to Ezekiel does not invalidate the point concerning their function.

28. 'Design and Themes', 208.

29. *Ezekiel*, 542.

30. *Theology*, 47-48.

31. *Ezekiel*, 2.345. Zimmerli identifies the original 'guidance vision' as comprising 40.1-37, 47-49, 41.1-4; 41.5-15a and 42.15-20 are early expansions by the same author, and 43.1-11(12) is likely also to be from this hand.

32. 'Planungen', 236.

33. The original integrity of these verses and their continuity with the foregoing is much debated. Bertholet, Hölscher, and Fohrer maintain that they are an addition; Zimmerli acknowledges only 'an element of uncertainty regarding the question of whether the Tora of 43.12 originally belonged to 43.1-11' (*Ezekiel*, 2.420). Talmon and Fishbane argue for the integrity of these verses, based on the chiastic parallelism to the introduction to the vision, 40.1-5 ('Aspects of Arrangement', 34-35). The issue of authorship does not directly affect my argument concerning the function of these verses.

34. Talmon and Fishbane link it with 42.15-20 (*ibid.*, 34).

35. Consistent with his view that chs. 40-48 form a self-contained unit, Eichrodt breaks the connection by omitting vv. 10aβb, 11aα as 'secondary insertions'.

36. *Theology*, 48.

37. See Pratt's suggestion that narratives should be classified as 'representatives' and therefore 'fall into the class whose primary point is thought-producing, representative or world-describing' (*Speech Act Theory*, 143). Her characterization modifies that of Searle, who sets the following criterion for identifying a 'representative' or 'assertive' speech act: 'The simplest test of an assertive is this: can you literally characterize it (inter alia) as true or false' (Searle, *Expression and Meaning*, 13). The problem with this view—mitigated, but not fully alleviated by Pratt—is that it lacks any implication of a creative dimension. While Searle allows for fictional utterances 'which suspend the normal operations of the rules relating illocutionary acts and the world' (*ibid.*, 67), he does not really consider the possibility that assertives might mediate new relations between the actual and the possible which cannot be judged in terms of truth or falsehood.

38. Niditch makes a similar point about Ezekiel's vision from the perspective of comparative religions. She claims that the Temple plan resembles the Tibetan mandala as a symbolic representation of the cosmos through which the mystic gains admittance to the sacred realm. The Buddhist visionaries, the author of Ezek. 40–48, the rabbis who engaged in mystical study of the *Merkavah* (Ezek. 1, though in an amplified form influenced by chs. 40–48)—'all of them not only experience a cosmos or have one revealed to them, but also create one themselves, whether it be in imagination, verbal description, or real materials. Perhaps it would be more accurate to say that they participate in the creation and recreation of a world. The building not only becomes a symbolization or an image of God's realm—whether it be his realm in the other world or on earth, and, in that way, a sign of the seer's special wisdom and status—but also indicates the seer's participation in the very process of world-creation' ('Ezekiel 40–48', 215).

39. Cooke, *Ezekiel*, 425; Zimmerli, 'Planungen', 236; Talmon, 'Literary Structuring', 325-26.

40. Zimmerli, *Ezekiel*, 2.419. Haran reads in וכתב a *waw explicativum* with the meaning: 'Bring these matters to their knowledge by having these matters written down in their presence; when the people become aware that these matters are committed to writing, they will learn them from the book' ('Law Code', 50). The closest equivalent to such a visual representation which has been found at Qumran is the pattern of concentric rectangles woven into the linen wrappings of the Temple scroll, which, by virtue of both function and the high degree of abstraction, certainly presupposes the prior existence of the text. See the comments by Grace Crowfoot in D. Barthélemy and J.T. Milik, *Discoveries in the Judaean Desert* (Oxford: Clarendon Press, 1955), 1.24-25; cf. Yadin, *Temple Scroll*, 1.153-54 (English version, 162-63).

41. See Haran: 'The prophetic 'experience' itself is surely confined here within the limits of literature, and the entire code is a literary-ecstatic work in the sense that it begins and ends within literary bounds. . . .[I]t is quite possible that, generally, in [Ezekiel's] case the quality of writer actually exceed that of orator. In the law-code it becomes truly pervasive and determinant (sic)' ('Law Code', 51). This is preferable to Zimmerli's attempt to distinguish between the direct deposit of ecstatic experience perceptible in ch. 43 and 'the infiltration of strong elements of reflection, even of graphic mediation on the visionary spectacle' in chs. 40–42 (*Ezekiel*, 2.412)—although he (somewhat contradictorily) designates chs. 40–42 as the 'basic guidance vision', and ch. 43 clearly presupposes its measurements.

42. *Ezekiel*, 2.346-47. Greenberg cites rabbinic tradition and 'some moderns' to the effect that the twenty-fifth year of exile was itself a Jubilee year (*Ezekiel*, 1.11).

43. The inference of human participation in accomplishment of the vision is a point on which Ezekiel's prophecy might well be distinguished from apocalyptic writings.

44. It is a weakness of Greenberg's defense of single authorship—though acknowledging that this probably occurred in stages—that he confines himself to a discussion of style and topical organization and does not treat questions of incompatible substance. Note, for example, the expression of horror that uncircumcised foreigners should have served as temple guards (44.6-14), of which 40.45 knows nothing (cf. also 3.6); the polemic sharply distinguishing between the Levites and the Zadokites (44.10-15), in contrast to earlier undifferentiated accusations against the priests (7.26; 22.26); and the allocation of land to priests (ch. 48), which seems to be prohibited in 44.28.

45. Zimmerli's concept of *Fortschreibung* suggests just this sort of successive building upon a basic stratum. He, in fact, draws a connection between the narrative elements of the book and the first stages of literary editing (*Ezekiel*, 1.68). This approach shows a better appreciation of the nature of narrative development than does Eichrodt's attempt to identify 'alien elements'.

46. I accept Zimmerli's judgment, based on considerations of style and content, that these verses constitute a separate unit by a later writer (*Ezekiel*, 2.374). It should be noted also that, in contrast to the basic vision, this is not a groundplan: the upper storeys of the outlying building are mentioned. Eichrodt designates only vv. 5-12 as 'an intrusive narrative' (*Ezekiel*, 546); however, the basic point about the addition's purpose is unaffected.

47. *Ezekiel*, 2.453.

48. The versions read the second-person plural; G.R. Driver refers the third-person form to the foreigners ('Ezekiel: Linguistic and Textual Problems', *Biblica* 35 [1954], 309).

49. Haran notes that 'geometric or geographical minutiae and legalistic niceties are *a priori* directed to readers, not to auditors' ('Law Code', 50).

## Notes to Chapter 6

1. *Prolegomena*, 59-60, 403-404.
2. *Prophecy and Canon*, 71.
3. Abraham Heschel, *The Prophets* (New York: Harper & Row, 1962).
4. See pp. 64f. above.
5. Frank M. Cross, *Canaanite Myth and Hebrew Epic* (Cambridge: Harvard University Press, 1973), 343. A related suggestion—unfortunately, not fully articulated—is that of Hammershaimb, who connects the demise of the characteristic pre-exilic prophecy of doom to the changing structure of Israelite society as a whole. His point seems to be that the exile ended the tension between old tribal values and the rise of an urban society which had generated the prophets' denunciations (*Some Aspects*, 109-12).
6. *History of Prophecy*, 182.
7. Crenshaw, *Prophetic Conflict*, 103-106; see also Wilson, *Prophecy and Society*, 307.
8. Such an 'internal' perspective already informs the work of David Petersen, who comments: 'Rather than speak about the end of Israelite prophecy, we should perhaps speak of the transition from classical prophecy to an organically connected but profoundly different enterprise' (*Late Israelite Prophecy*, 6). He highlights Deutero-Isaiah and Trito-Isaiah as transitional figures in the passage between the political-religious model of classical prophecy, oriented toward the monarchy, and a new kind of text-oriented prophecy, represented by Deutero-Zechariah, Joel, and Malachi. Although I differ from his view that Ezekiel is to be located wholly within the former model ('Israelite Prophecy', 72), his work is important for understanding the further development of the shift treated here.
9. This passage is usually assigned a post-exilic date; William Holladay suggests the middle of the fifth century (*Jeremiah* [Hermeneia, Philadelphia: Fortress Press, 1986], 1.649; cf. Petersen, *Late Exilic Prophecy*, 32).
10. *History of Prophecy*, 182.
11. *Prophecy and Society*, 308.
12. This perception finds expression in the famous dictum ascribed to Rabbi Abdimi of Haifa: 'Since the day when the Temple was destroyed, prophecy has been taken from the prophets and given to the wise (BT *Baba Batra* 12a; cf. Tosefta *Sota* 13.2). The rabbinic 'dogma' about the end of prophecy in Israel is a statement, not about the phenomenon of inspired speech itself, but about the kind of discourse which was recognized as authoritative in Israel. The teaching is concerned with the formation of a

canon: it distinguishes the age of the prophets from that of the wise on the basis of the kind of texts associated with each. So R. Leivestad: 'The rabbinic claim that prophecy is at an end organically coheres with the concept of a canon' ('Das Dogma von der Prophetenlosen Zeit', *New Testament Studies* 19 [1972/73], 290). See also John Barton, *Oracles of God*, 108-110; Morton Smith, *Palestinian Parties and Politics that Shaped the Old Testament* [New York: Columbia University Press, 1971], 118).

13. Waldemar Janzen suggests something of such a reciprocal causality, although with a different focus. He considers that the prophets began to record their message in despair of evoking from the people an immediate response, and that this in turn lessened the urgency to address the present populace ('Withholding the Word', *Traditions in Transformation*, ed. B. Halpern and J. Levenson [Winona Lake: Eisenbrauns, 1981], 110).

14. *Prolegomena*, 403.

15. *Prophecy and Canon*, 8.

16. It is an interesting point of connection between the two groups that both exilic prophets, like the editors of the Pentateuch, look to the distant past and find in the pre-state period a key for their (albeit very different) understandings of the present. This is evident in all of Ezekiel's historical reviews and in the Second Isaiah's preference for the Exodus theme over that of the Davidic promise.

17. *Prophecy and Canon*, 94.

18. While (as indicated by the quotation heading this chapter) Jacques Derrida represents this 'death of the author' as a general phenomenon, Michel Foucault sees it more as an effect of modern literary conventions, which reverse the earlier notion that a work immortalizes its creator: '. . . we find the link between writing and death manifested in the total effacement of the individual characteristics of the writer; the quibbling and confrontations that a writer generates between himself and his text cancel out the signs of his particular individuality. If we wish to know the writer in our day, it will be through the singularity of his absence and in his link to death, which has transformed him into a victim of his own writing' (*Language, Counter-Memory, Practice*, ed. Donald F. Bouchard [Ithaca: Cornell University Press, 1977], 116).

19. *Old Testament Theology*, 2.45.

20. It is interesting that the burden of this prophet's message and the source of his anguish seems to be the delay in fulfilment of the prophetic promises and visions, and that in so far as any solution to this dilemma is offered, it lies in the direction of inscription (2.2-3).

21. *Old Testament Theology*, 264-65. Von Rad's suggestion that 'the Book of Ezekiel is practically a long prophetic autobiography' (*Old Testament Theology*, 2.265) runs quite contrary to the case I have presented concerning the purpose of the first-person narrative frame.

22. *Ezekiel*, 1.18.

23. The indefinite אלהם ('to them', 1.3) receives no further specification. The only fragment of speech which stands outside an address to the prophet is the second-person statement in 1.2, but this is better construed as a summary of the message to follow than as a direct address to the people.

24. 'Prophecy to Apocalyptic', 48.

25. Petersen argues that 'Zechariah's visions comprise the doing of theology', and that their structure is to be understood specifically as a revision of Ezekiel's plan for the restoration community (*Haggai and Zechariah*, 115-19).

26. 'Prophecy to Apocalyptic', 71.

27. Petersen argues against reading Isa. 40.6 autobiographically (repointing MT's ואמר as a first-person singular form) and instead follows 1QIsa[a] in reading ואומרה, taken as a Qal feminine singular participle, whose subject is Zion-Jerusalem (*Late Israelite Prophecy*, 20-21).

28. The LXX takes this to be the case, as do many moderns (e.g. Koch, *Prophets*, 2.178); but see Childs's argument to the contrary (*Introduction*, 492-94).

29. *Prophets*, 2.181-82.

30. It was not, of course, only the specifically prophetic texts which were available for such an encounter. Note the transformation of the technical term for seeking a prophetic oracle, דרש את יי ('inquire of YHWH') into דרש את תורת-יי ('inquire of the Torah of YHWH') in Ezra 7.10.

31. Carroll treats the phenomenon of 'corrective prophecy' as part of a self-reflective dialogue within the prophetic tradition which evolved during the post-exilic period (*When Prophecy Failed*, 177-79). See also Petersen on the Isaiah traditionists (*Late Israelite Prophecy*, 25-27) and Koch on the 'relativization' of the Second Isaiah's prophecy by the Third Isaiah, and of Haggai's and Zechariah's oracles by Malachi (*Prophets*, 2.153-59, 175-78).

32. See Blenkinsopp, 'Interpretation', 24-25.

33. Kugel sees Ps. 111.2b as a reference to this process of consulting the written record of God's deeds, which may be 'scrutinized [*derushim*] in their every detail' ('Two Introductions', 137).

# BIBLIOGRAPHY

Abrahams, Roger D. 'Introductory Remarks to a Rhetorical Theory of Folklore', *Journal of American Folklore* 81 (1968): 143-58.

Ackroyd, Peter R. *Exile and Restoration*, Philadelphia: Westminster Press, 1981.

Albright, W.F. 'King Joiachin in Exile', *Biblical Archaeologist* 5 (1942): 49-55.

Barr, James. 'Reading a Script without Vowels', *Writing without Letters*, ed. W. Haas, Manchester: Manchester University Press; Totowa, NJ: Rowman & Littlefield, 1976, 71-100.

Barthes, Roland, 'An Introduction to the Structural Analysis of Narrative', *NLH* 8 (1976/77): 237-72.

Barton, John. *Oracles of God: Perceptions of Ancient Prophecy in Israel after the Exile*, London: Darton, Longman & Todd, 1986.

Berggren, Douglas. 'The Use and Abuse of Metaphor', *Review of Metaphysics* 16 (1962-63): 237-58, 450-72.

Berry, George Ricker. 'The Title of Ez $(1_{1-3})$', *JBL* 51 (1932): 54-57.

Bertholet, Alfred. *Hesekiel* (Handbuch zum Alten Testament 13), Tübingen: J.C.B. Mohr, 1936.

—*Der Verfassungsentwurf des Hesekiel in seiner religionsgeschichtlichen Bedeutung*, Freiburg: J.C.B. Mohr, 1896.

*Biblical Archaeology Today* (Proceedings of the International Congress on Biblical Archaeology, Jerusalem, April 1984), Jerusalem: Israel Exploration Society, 1985.

Blenkinsopp, Joseph. *A History of Prophecy in Israel*, Philadelphia: Westminster Press, 1983.

—'Interpretation and the Tendency to Sectarianism: An Aspect of Second Temple History', *Jewish and Christian Self-Definition*, ed. E.P. Sanders, Philadelphia: Fortress Press, 1981, 2:1-16.

—*Prophecy and Canon*, Notre Dame: University of Notre Dame Press, 1977.

Booth, Wayne. 'Metaphor as Rhetoric', *Critical Inquiry* 5 (1978): 49-72.

—*The Rhetoric of Fiction*, Chicago: Universiy of Chicago Press, 2nd edn, 1983.

Boyarin, Daniel, and David Stern, 'An Exchange on the Mashal', *Prooftexts* 5 (1985): 269-80.

Brin, Gershon, *Studies in the Book of Ezekiel* (Hebrew), Haifa: Hakibutz Hameuhad, 1975.

Broome, Edwin C. 'Ezekiel's Abnormal Personality', *JBL* 65 (1946): 277-92.

Brownlee, William. '"Son of Man Set Your Face", Ezekiel the Refugee Prophet", *HUCA* 54 (1983): 83-110.

Bruss, Elizabeth W. 'Models and Metaphors for Narrative Analysis', *Centrum* 2/1 (1974): 14-41.

Burhenn, Herbert. 'Narrative Explanation and Redescription', *Canadian Journal of Philosophy* 3 (1974): 419-25.

Burrows, Millar. *The Literary Relations of Ezekiel*, Philadelphia: Jewish Publications Society Press, 1925.

Carley, Keith W. *Ezekiel among the Prophets* (Studies in Biblical Theology, II/31), Naperville, IL: Alec R. Allenson, Inc., 1974 or 1975.

Carroll, Robert P. *When Prophecy Failed: Cognitive Dissonance in the Prophetic Traditions of the Old Testament*, New York: Seabury Press, 1979.

Cassem, Ned H. 'Ezekiel's Psychotic Personality: Reservations on the Use of the Couch for Biblical Personalities', *The Word in the World* (FS F.L. Moriarty), ed. R.J. Clifford and G.W. MacRae, Cambridge: Weston College Press, 1973, 59-69.

Chatman, Seymour. 'Toward a Theory of Narrative', *NLH* 6 (1974/75): 295-318.

Chaytor, H.J. *From Script to Print*, London: Sidgwick & Jackson, 1966.

Childs, Brevard S. 'The Canonical Shape of the Prophetic Literature', *Interpretation* 32 (1978): 46-55.

—*Introduction to the Old Testament as Scripture*, Philadelphia: Fortress Press, 1979.

Clements, R.E. 'The Ezekiel Tradition: Prophecy in a Time of Crisis', *Israel's Prophetic Tradition* (FS Peter R. Ackroyd), ed. R. Coggins, A. Phillips, and M. Knibb, Cambridge: Cambridge University Press, 1982, 119-36.

Cohen, Ted. 'Metaphor and the Cultivation of Intimacy', *Critical Inquiry* 5 (1978): 3-12.

Cooke, G.A. *A Critical and Exegetical Commentary on the Book of Ezekiel* (ICC), New York: Charles Scribner's Sons, 1937.

Cornill, Carl Heinrich. *Das Buch des Propheten Ezechiel*, Leipzig: J.C. Hinrichs, 1886.

—'Ezekiel, Book of', *Jewish Encyclopedia*, 1916, 5:316-18.

Crenshaw, James. 'Education in Ancient Israel', *JBL* 104 (1985): 601-15.

—*Prophetic Conflict*, Berlin: Walter de Gruyter, 1971.

Cross, F.M. 'The Origin and Early Evolution of the Alphabet', *Eretz Israel* 8 (1967): 8-24.

Curnow, Ann. 'Analysis of Written Style - An Imperative for Readable Translations', *READ* 14 (1979): 75-83.

Davies, W.D., & Louis Finkelstein, eds. *The Cambridge History of Judaism*, Cambridge: Cambridge University Press, 1984.

Day-Lewis, C. *The Poetic Image*, London: Jonathan Cape, 1947.

Demsky, Aaron. 'Education', *Encyclopaedia Judaica*, 1971, 6:381-98.

—'Literacy in Israel and among Neighboring People in the Biblical Period', Ph.D. dissertation, Hebrew University in Jerusalem, 1976.

—'Writing', *Encyclopaedia Judaica*, 1971, 16:654-65.

Dinor, Ben Zion. 'Education' (Hebrew), *Encyclopedia Mikra'it*, 1958, 3:114-22.

Eaton, Marcia M. 'Liars, Ranters, and Dramatic Speakers', *Language and Aesthetics*, ed. Benjamin Tilghman, Lawrence: University Press of Kansas, 1973, 43-63.

Egan, Kieran. 'What is a Plot?', *NLH* 9 (1977/78): 455-73.

Eichrodt, Walther. *Ezekiel* (OTL), Philadelphia: Westminster Press, 1970.

Eliezer of Beaugency. *Kommentar zu Ezechiel und den XII kleinen Propheten* (Hebrew), Warsaw: A.Y. Poznanski, 1909.

Engnell, Ivan. *A Rigid Scrutiny*, ed. John J. Willis, Nashville: Vanderbilt University Press, 1969.

Ewald, G.H.A. von. *Commentary on the Prophets of the Old Testament*, London: Williams & Norgate, 1880 (German original, Stuttgart: A. Krabbe, 1840-41).

Finegan, Jack. 'The Chronology of Ezekiel', *JBL* 69 (1950): 61-66.

Finnegan, Ruth. 'How Oral is Oral Literature?', *Bulletin of the School of Oriental and African Studies* 37 (1974): 52-64.

—'Literacy versus Non-Literacy: The Great Divide?', *Modes of Thought*, ed. Robin Horton & Ruth Finnegan, London: Faber & Faber, 1973, 112-44.

Fishbane, Michael. *Biblical Interpretation in Ancient Israel*, Oxford: Clarendon Press, 1985.

—'Sin and Judgment in the Prophecies of Ezekiel', *Interpretation* 38 (1984): 131-50.

Fohrer, Georg. *Ezechiel* (HAT 13), Tübingen: J.C.B. Mohr, 1955.

—*Die Hauptprobleme des Buches Ezechiel* (BZAW 72), Berlin: Töpelmann, 1952.

—*Die Symbolischen Handlungen der Propheten* (ATANT 54), Zurich: Zwingli Verlag, 1953.

Fontaine, Carole. 'Proverb Performance in the Hebrew Bible', *JSOT* 32 (1985): 87-103.

—*Traditional Sayings of the Old Testament* (Bible and Literature Series 5), Sheffield: Almond Press, 1982.

Fox, Michael. 'The Rhetoric of Ezekiel's Vision of the Valley of the Bones', *HUCA* 51 (1980): 1-15.

Freedman, D.N. 'The Book of Ezekiel', *Interpretation* 8 (1954): 446-71.

Freedy, K.S., & D.B. Redford, 'The Dates in Ezekiel in Relation to Biblical, Babylonian, and Egyptian Resources', *JAOS* 90 (1970): 462-85.

Gandz, Solomon. 'Oral Tradition in the Bible', *Jewish Studies in Memory of George A. Kohut*, ed. Salo Baron & Alexander Marx, New York: Alexander Kohut Memorial Foundation, 1935, 248-69.

Garscha, Jörg. *Studien zum Ezechielbuch* (Europäische Hochschulschriften 23), Bern: Herbert Lang; Frankfurt: Peter Lang, 1974.

Gasparov, Boris. 'The Narrative Text as an Act of Communication', *NLH* 9 (1977/78): 245-61.

Gerhardsson, Birger. *Memory and Manuscript*, Uppsala: Almqvist & Wiksells, 1961.

Gitay, Yehoshua. 'Deutero-Isaiah: Oral or Written?', *JBL* 99 (1980): 185-97.

Goody, Jack. *The Domestication of the Savage Mind*, Cambridge: Cambridge University Press, 1977.

—'Literacy, Criticism, and the Growth of Knowledge', *Culture and its Creators*, ed. Joseph Ben-David & Tracy Nichols Clark, Chicago: University of Chicago Press, 1977, 226-43.

Goody, Jack, and Ian Watt. 'The Consequences of Literacy', *Literacy in Traditional Societies*, ed. Jack Goody, Cambridge: Cambridge University Press, 1968, 27-68.

Greenberg, Moshe. 'The Citations in the Book of Ezekiel as a Background for the Prophecies' (Hebrew), *Bet Mikra* 50 (1972): 273-78.

—'The Design and Themes of Ezekiel's Program of Restoration', *Interpretation* 38 (1984): 181-208.

—'Ezekiel', *Encyclopaedia Judaica*, 1971, 6:1078-95.

—*Ezekiel* (Anchor Bible), Garden City: Doubleday, 1983-.

—'Ezekiel 17 and the Policy of Psammetichus II', *JBL* 76 (1957): 304-309.

—'Prolegomenon', in C.C. Torrey, *Pseudo-Ezekiel and the Original Prophecy and Critical Articles*, New York: Ktav, 1970, xi-xxix.

—'The Vision of Jerusalem in Ezekiel 8-11: A Holistic Interpretation', *The Divine Helmsman*, ed. James Crenshaw & Samuel Sandmel, New York: Ktav, 1980, 143-63.

Greene, William Chase. 'The Spoken and the Written Word', *Harvard Studies in Classical Philology* 60 (1951): 23-59.

Gunkel, Hermann. 'Allegorie im A.T. und Judentum', *Religion in Geschichte und Gegenwart*, Tübingen: J.C.B. Mohr, 1909, 1:354-55.

170     *Swallowing the Scroll*

—'The Israelite Prophecy from the Time of Amos', *Twentieth Century Theology in the Making*, ed. Jaroslav Pelikan, New York: Harper & Row, 1969, 1:48-75.

—'Die Propheten als Schriftsteller und Dichter', *Die Schriften des Alten Testaments* 2/2, Göttingen: Vandenhoeck & Ruprecht, 1915, xxxvi-lxxii.

Gunneweg, Antonius. *Mündliche und schriftliche Tradition der vorexilischen Prophetenbücher*, Göttingen: Vandenhoeck & Ruprecht, 1959.

Hallo, W.W. 'New Viewpoints on Cuneiform Literature', *IEJ* 12 (1962): 13-26.

Hammershaimb, Erling. *Some Aspects of Old Testament Prophecy from Isaiah to Malachi*, Copenhagen: Rosenkilde og Bagger, 1966.

Hanson, Paul D. *The Dawn of Apocalyptic: The Historical and Sociological Roots of Jewish Apocalyptic Eschatology*, Philadelphia: Fortress Press, 2nd edn, 1979.

Haran, Menahem. 'The Law Code of Ezekiel XL-XLVIII and its Relation to the Priestly School', *HUCA* 50 (1979): 45-71.

Havelock, Eric A. *Preface to Plato*, Cambridge: Belnap Press of Harvard University Press, 1963.

—*Prologue to Greek Literacy*, Cincinnati: University of Cincinnato, 1971.

Havelock, Eric A., & Jackson P. Hershbell, *Communication Arts in the Ancient World*, New York: Hastings House, 1978.

Henige, David P. *The Chronology of Oral Tradition*, Oxford: Clarendon Press, 1974.

Herner, Sven. 'Erziehung und Unterricht in Israel', *Oriental Studies Dedicated to Paul Haupt*, Baltimore: Johns Hopkins Press, 1926, 58-66.

Herntrich, Volkmar. *Ezechielprobleme*, Giessen: Töpelmann, 1933.

Herrmann, Johannes. *Ezechiel, übersetzt und erklärt*, Leipzig: A. Deichert, 1924.

—*Ezechielstudien* (BWAT 2), Leipzig: Hinrichs, 1908.

Hirsch, E.D. Jr. *The Philosophy of Composition*, Chicago: University of Chicago Press, 1977.

Hitzig, Ferdinand. *Der Prophet Ezechiel erklärt*, Leipzig: S. Hirzel, 1847.

Hölscher, Gustav. *Hesekiel, der Dichter und das Buch* (BZAW 39), Giessen: Töpelmann, 1924.

Hossfeld, Frank. *Untersuchungen zu Komposition und Theologie des Ezechielbuches* (Forschung zur Bibel 20), Würzburg: Echter Verlag, 1977.

Irwin, William. *The Problem of Ezekiel*, Chicago: University of Chicago Press, 1943.

—'The Problem of Ezekiel Today: A Study in Methodology', *Doron: Hebraic Studies*, ed. Israel Naamani & David Rudavsky, New York: National Association of Professors of Hebrew, 1965, 139-74.

Iser, Wolfgang. 'Indeterminacy and the Reader's Response in Prose Fiction', *Aspects of Narrative*, ed. J. Hillis Miller, New York: Columbia University Press, 1971, 1-45.

Jousse, Marcel. *La Manducation de la Parole* (*L'Anthropologie du Geste*, vol. 2), Paris: Gallimard, 1975.

Kaufmann, Yehezkel. *The Religion of Israel*, trans. Moshe Greenberg, Chicago: University of Chicago Press, 1960.

Kelber, Werner. *The Oral and Written Gospel*, Philadelphia: Fortress Press, 1983.

Knight, Douglas. *Rediscovering the Traditions of Israel* (SBL Dissertation Series 9), Missoula, MT: Scholars Press, 1973.

—(ed.). *Tradition and Theology in the Old Testament*, Philadelphia: Fortress Press, 1977.

Koch, Klaus. *The Prophets*, Philadelphia: Fortress Press, 1982.

Komlosh, Yehuda. 'The Silence of Ezekiel at the Beginning of His Prophecy' (Hebrew), *Zer Ligevurot* (Shazar Jubilee Volume), Jerusalem: Israel Society for Biblical Research, 1973, 279-83.

Kraetzschmar, Richard. *Das Buch Ezekiel* (Handkommentar zum Alten Testament III/3), Göttingen: Vandenhoeck & Ruprecht, 1900.

Kugel, James. 'Two Introductions to Midrash', *Prooftexts* 3 (1983): 131-55.

Labov, William, and Joshua Waletzky. 'Narrative Analysis: Oral Versions of Personal Experience', *Essays in the Verbal and Visual Arts: Proceedings of the 1966 Annual Spring Meeting of the American Ethnological Society*, ed. June Helm, Seattle: University of Washington Press, 1967.

Laessøe, J. 'Literacy and Oral Tradition in Ancient Mesopotamia', *Studia Orientalia Ioanni Pedersen*, Hauniae: Einar Munksgaard, 1953, 205-18.

Lambert, W.G. *Babylonian Wisdom Literature*, Oxford: Clarendon Press, 1960.

Lamparter, Helmut. *Zum Wächter bestellt: Der Prophet Hesekiel*, Stuttgart: Calwer Verlag, 1968.

Lang, Bernhard. *Kein Aufstand in Jerusalem*, Stuttgart: Verlag Katholisches Bibelwerk, 1978.

—*Monotheism and the Prophetic Minority: An Essay in Biblical History and Sociology* (Social World of Biblical Antiquity 1), Sheffield: Almond Press, 1983.

—'Schule und Unterricht im alten Israel', *La Sagesse de l'Ancien Testament* (BETL 51), ed. M. Gilbert, Gembloux: Duculot, 1979: 186-201.

Langer, Susanne. *Feeling and Form*, London: Routledge & Kegan Paul, 1953.

Lemaire, André. *Les Écoles et la formation de la Bible dans l'Ancien Israel*, Göttingen: Vandenhoeck & Ruprecht, 1981.

—'Sagesse et Écoles', *VT* 34 (1984): 270-81.

Lemke, Werner. 'Life in the Present and Hope for the Future', *Interpretation* 38 (1984): 165-80.

Levenson, Jon D. *Theology of the Program of Restoration of Ezekiel 40-48* (Harvard Semitic Monograph 10), Missoula, MT: Scholars Press, 1976.

Lindblom, J. *Prophecy in Ancient Israel*, Philadelphia: Fortress Press, 1962.

Lods, Adolphe. *The Prophets and the Rise of Judaism*, London: Routledge & Kegan Paul, 1937.

Ludwig, Theodore M. 'Remember Not the Former Things', *Transitions and Transformations in the History of Religions*, ed. F.E. Reynolds & T.M. Ludwig, Leiden: Brill, 1980, 25-55.

Lust, J., ed. *Ezekiel and his Book* (BETL 74), Leuven: Leuven University Press, 1986.

Malamat, A. 'The Twilight of Judah', *VTSup* 28 (Edinburgh, 1974): 123-45.

Matejka, Ladislav, and Krystyna Pomorska. *Readings in Russian Poetics*, Cambridge: MIT Press, 1971.

Mitchell, W.J.T., ed. *On Narrative*, Chicago: University of Chicago Press, 1981.

Moskovitz, Yehiel. *The Book of Ezekiel* (Hebrew), Jerusalem: Mossad Harav Kook, 1985.

Mowinckel, Sigmund. *Prophecy and Tradition*, Oslo: I Kommisjon Hos Jacob Dybwad, 1946.

Naveh, Joseph. 'A Paleographic Note on the Distribution of the Hebrew Script', *HTR* 61 (1968): 68-74.

Newsom, Carol. 'A Maker of Metaphors—Ezekiel's Oracles Against Tyre', *Interpretation* 38 (1984): 151-64.

Niditch, Susan. 'Ezekiel 40–48 in a Visionary Context', *CBQ* 48 (1986): 208-24.

Nielsen, Eduard. *Oral Tradition*, Naperville, IL: Alec R. Allenson, 1954.

North, Robert. 'Prophecy to Apocalyptic via Zechariah', *VTSup* 22 (Uppsala, 1971): 47-71.

Oded, Bustaney. 'Judah and the Exile', *Israelite and Judaean History*, ed. John H. Hayes & J. Maxwell Miller, Philadelphia: Westminster Press, 1977, 435-88.

Ogden, Charles, and I.A. Richards. *The Meaning of Meaning*, New York: Harcourt, Brace, 8th edn, 1956.

Oliver, Curtis F. 'Some Aspects of Literacy in Ancient India', *The Quarterly Newsletter of the Laboratory of Comparative Human Cognition*, 1/4 (1979): 57-62.

Olson, David R. 'From Utterance to Text: The Bias of Language in Speech and Writing', *Harvard Educational Review* 47 (1977): 257-81.

—'Some Social Aspects of Meaning in Oral and Written Language', *The Social Foundations of Language and Thought*, ed. David R. Olson, New York: W.W. Norton, 1980, 90-108.

Olson, David R., Nancy Torrance, and Angela Hildyard, eds. *Literary, Language, and Learning*, Cambridge: Cambridge University Press, 1985.

Ong, Walter J. *Interfaces of the Word: Studies in the Evolution of Consciousness and Culture*, Ithaca: Cornell University Press, 1977.

—'Oral Remembering and Narrative Structures', *Analyzing Discourse: Text and Talk* (Georgetown University Round Table on Languages and Linguistics, 1981), Deborah Tannen, ed., Washington, D.C.: Georgetown University Press, 1982, 12-24.

—*Orality and Literacy: The Technologizing of the Word*, London: Methuen, 1982.

—*The Presence of the Word*, New Haven: Yale University Press, 1967.

—*Rhetoric, Romance, and Technology*, Ithaca: Cornell University Press, 1971.

Orelli, Conrad von. *Das Buch Ezechiel*, Munich: Ch. Beck, 1896.

Ortony, Andrew, ed. *Metaphor and Thought*, Cambridge: Cambridge University Press, 1979.

—'Why Metaphors Are Necessary and Not Just Nice', *Educational Theory* 25 (1975): 45-53.

Parunak, H. Van Dyke. 'The Literary Architecture of Ezekiel's *Mar'ôt 'Elōhîm*', *JBL* 99 (1980): 61-74.

Pattison, Robert. *On Literacy: The Politics of the Word from Homer to the Age of Rock*, London/New York: Oxford University Press, 1982.

Perelman, Chaim. *The Realm of Rhetoric*, Notre Dame: University of Notre Dame, 1982.

Perelmann, Chaim, & L. Olbrechts-Tyteca. *The New Rhetoric: A Treatise on Argumentation*, Notre Dame: University of Notre Dame, 1969.

Petersen, David L. *Haggai and Zechariah 1–8: A Commentary*, London: SCM Press, 1984.

—'Israelite Prophecy and Prophetic Traditions in the Exilic and Post-Exilic Periods', Ph. D. dissertation, Yale University, 1972.

—*Late Israelite Prophecy: Studies in Deutero-Prophetic Literature and in Chronicles* (SBL Monograph Series 23), Missoula, MT: Scholars Press, 1977.

Ploeg, J. van der. 'La Rôle de la Tradition Orale dans la Transmission du Texte de l'Ancien Testament', *RB* 54 (1947): 5-41.

Polk, Timothy. 'Paradigms, Parables, and Mešālîm: On Reading the Māšāl in Scripture', *CBQ* 45 (1983): 564-83.

Pratt, Mary Louise. *Toward a Speech Act Theory of Literary Discourse*, Bloomington: Indiana University Press, 1977.

Rabenau, Konrad von. 'Die Form des Rätsels im Buche Hesekiel', *Gottes ist der Orient* (FS Otto Eissfeldt), Berlin: Evangelische Verlagsanstalt, 1957, 129-31.

Rad, Gerhard von. *Old Testament Theology*, New York: Harper & Row, 1962.

—*Wisdom in Israel*, Nashville: Abingdon Press, 1972.

Reventlow, H. Graf. *Wächter über Israel* (BZAW 82), Berlin: Töpelmann, 1962.

Ricoeur, Paul. 'Biblical Hermeneutics', *Semeia* 4 (1975): 29-148.

—*The Conflict of Interpretations: Essays in Hermeneutics*, Evanston: Northwestern University Press, 1974.

—*Hermeneutics and the Human Sciences*, Cambridge: Cambridge University Press, 1981.

—*Interpretation Theory: Discourse and the Surplus of Meaning*, Fort Worth: Texas Christian University Press, 1976.

—*The Symbolism of Evil*, New York: Harper & Row, 1967.

—*Time and Narrative*, Chicago: University of Chicago Press, 1984-86.

Robinson, H. Wheeler. *Two Hebrew Prophets*, London: Lutterworth Press, 1948.

Rowley, H.H. 'The Book of Ezekiel in Modern Study', *Men of God*, London: Thomas Nelson, 1963: 169-210.

Sanders, James A. 'Adaptable for Life: The Nature and Function of Canon', *Magnalia Dei: Essays on the Bible and Archaeology in Memory of G. Ernest Wright*, ed. Frank M. Cross *et al.*, Garden City: Doubleday, 1976, 531-60.

—'Hermeneutics', *Interpreter's Dictionary of the Bible, Supplement*, 1976, 402-407.

—'Hermeneutics in True and False Prophecy', *Canon and Authority*, ed. G.W. Coats & B.O. Long, Philadelphia: Fortress Press, 1977, 21-41.

Scholes, Robert and Robert Kellogg. *The Nature of Narrative*, London/New York: Oxford University Press, 1966.

Scollon, Ron, and Suzanne Scollon. 'Literacy as Focused Interaction', *The Quarterly Newsletter of the Laboratory of Comparative Human Cognition* 2/2 (1980): 26-29.

Scribner, Sylvia, and Michael Cole. 'Literacy without Schooling: Testing for Intellectual Effects', *Harvard Educational Review* 48 (1978): 448-61.

Scheub, Harold. 'Oral Narrative Process and the Use of Models', *NLH* 77 (1974): 353-77.

Searle, John R. *Expression and Meaning*, Cambridge: Cambridge University Press, 1979.

Seidel, Moshe. 'Parallels between the Book of Isaiah and the Book of Psalms' (Hebrew), *Sinai* 38 (1956): 149-72.

Seitel, Peter. 'Proverbs: A Social Use of Metaphor', *Folklore Genres*, ed. Dan Ben-Amos, Austin: University of Texas Press, 1976, 125-43.

Smend, Rudolf. *Der Prophet Ezechiel*, Leipzig: S. Hirzel, 1880.

Smith, James. *The Book of the Prophet Ezekiel*, London: SPCK, 1931.

Smith, Morton. *Palestinian Parties and Politics that Shaped the Old Testament*, New York: Columbia University Press, 1971.

Soskice, Janet Martin. *Metaphor and Religious Language*, Oxford: Clarendon Press, 1985.

—'Theological Realism', *The Rationality of Religious Belief: Essays in Honor of Basil Mitchell*, ed. William J. Abraham and Steven W. Holtzer, Oxford: Clarendon Press, 1987, 105-19.

Spiegel, Shalom. 'Ezekiel or Pseudo-Ezekiel?', *HTR* 24 (1931): 245-321.

Stern, David. 'Rhetoric and Midrash: The Case of the Mashal', *Prooftexts* 1 (1981): 261-77.

—'The Role of the Mashal in Rabbinic Literature' (Hebrew), *Jerusalem Studies in Hebrew Literature* 7 (1985): 90-102.

Swift, Fletcher Harper. *Educating in Ancient Israel*, Chicago: The Open Court, 1919.

Talmon, Shemaryahu. 'Literary Structuring in the Book of Ezekiel' (Hebrew), *Bet Mikra* 63 (1975): 315-27.

Talmon, Shemaryahu, and Michael Fishbane. 'Aspects of the Arrangement of Sections in the Book of Ezekiel' (Hebrew), *Tarbiz* 42 (1972/73): 27-41.

—'The Structuring of Biblical Books: Studies in the Book of Ezekiel', *ASTI* 10 (1976): 129-53.

Tannen, Deborah, ed. *Spoken and Written Language*, Norwood, NJ: Ablex, 1982.

Thomas, D. Winton. 'The Sixth Century B.C.: A Creative Epoch in the History of Israel', *JSS* 6 (1951): 33-46.

Torrey, Charles Cutler. *Pseudo-Ezekiel and the Original Prophecy*, New Haven: Yale University Press, 1930.

Tur-Sinai, N.H. *The Simple Meaning of Scripture* (Hebrew), Jerusalem: Kiryat Sepher, 1967.

Urbach, Ephraim E. 'When Did Prophecy Cease?' (Hebrew), *Tarbiz* 17 (1946): 1-11.

Vogt, Ernst, 'Die Lähmung und Stummheit des Propheten Ezechiel', *Wort–Gebot–Glaube* (FS Walther Eichrodt), Zurich: Zwingli Verlag, 1970, 87-100.

Weidner, Ernst F. 'Jojachin, König von Juda, in babylonischen Keilschrifttexten', *Mélanges syriens offerts à M. René Dussaud* (Bibliothèque Archéologique et Historique $30^{1-2}$), Paris: Geuthner, 1939, 923-35.

Weiss, Raphael. 'On Chiasmus in Scripture' (Hebrew), *Bet Mikra* 7 (1962): 46-51.

Wellhausen, Julius. *Prolegomena to the History of Ancient Israel*, Gloucester, MA: Peter Smith, 1983 (German original, Berlin: G. Reimer, 1878).

Wevers, John W. *Ezekiel* (Century Bible), London: Thomas Nelson, 1969.

Wheelwright, Philip. *Metaphor and Reality*, Bloomington: Indiana University Press, 1962.

Whitehead, Alfred North. *Religion in the Making*, New York: Macmillan, 1930.

Widengren, Geo. *Literary and Psychological Aspects of the Hebrew Prophets*, Uppsala: A.-B. Lundequistska Bokhandeln, 1948.

Williams, James G. *Those Who Ponder Proverbs* (Bible and Literature Series 2), Sheffield: Almond Press, 1981.

Wilson, Robert R. 'An Interpretation of Ezekiel's Dumbness', *VT* 22 (1972): 91-104.

—*Prophecy and Society in Ancient Israel*, Philadelphia: Fortress Press, 1980.

—'Prophecy in Crisis: The Call of Ezekiel', *Interpretation* 38 (1984): 117-30.

Wiseman, D.J. 'Books in the Ancient Near East and in the Old Testament', *Cambridge History of the Bible*, ed. P.R. Ackroyd & C.F. Evans, Cambridge: Cambridge University Press, 1970, 1:30-48.

Wolff, Hans Walter. 'The Understanding of History in the Old Testament Prophets', *Essays in Old Testament Hermeneutics*, ed. Claus Westermann, Atlanta: John Knox Press, 1963, 336-55.

—*Das Zitat im Prophetenspruch*, Munich: Chr. Kaiser, 1937.

Yadin, Yigael. *The Temple Scroll* (Hebrew), Jerusalem: Hebrew University Institute of Archaeology, 1977 (abridged English version, New York: Random House, 1985).

Yaron, Kalman. 'The Dirge over the King of Tyre', *ASTI* 3 (1964): 28-57.

Zimmerli, Walther. *Ezekiel* (Hermeneia), Philadelphia: Fortress Press, 1983 (German original [BKAT 13], Neukirchen-Vluyn: Neukirchener Verlag, 1969).

—'Israel im Buche Ezechiel', *VT* 8 (1952): 75-90.

—'The Message of the Prophet Ezekiel', *Interpretation* 23 (1969): 131-57.

—'Planungen für den Wiederaufbau nach der Katastrophe von 587', *VT* 18 (1968): 229-55.

—'The Special Form- and Traditio-Historical Character of Ezekiel's Prophecy', *VT* 15 (1965): 515-27.

—'The Word of God in the Book of Ezekiel', *History and Hermeneutic*, ed. Robert W. Funk, New York: Harper & Row, 1967.

# INDEXES

## INDEX OF BIBLICAL REFERENCES

# INDEX OF AUTHORS